Touring the
Cabot Trail
and beyond

4th EDITION

SUSAN BIAGI

PHOTOGRAPHY BY KEITH VAUGHAN

FORMAC PUBLISHING COMPANY LIMITED
HALIFAX

ACKNOWLEDGEMENTS

I would like to thank the following people for their help:

Jocelyne Quann, former naturalist at the Cape Breton Highlands National Park, for her careful review of the park sections of the manuscript, as well as her unfailing good humour and generosity.

Dr. Robert Morgan, for graciously permitting us to use the photographs in the University College of Cape Breton's Beaton Archives.

Amy Black, publishing assistant at Formac, Peggy McCalla, production coordinator, and Elizabeth Eve, copy editor, for their work in bringing the manuscript to its present form.

Jim Lorimer, President of Formac, for giving me the freedom to follow my instincts and the confidence to share my discoveries.

I would also like to thank my husband, Mark Biagi, for cheerfully climbing all those mountains, and my sister Linda Young, for a memorable day of moose-sightings.

— S.B.

All photographs are by Keith Vaughan, except where noted below. Top=T, Bottom=B, Right=R, Left=L
Cape Breton Highlands National Park: pp.13 T, 31 B, 39 T&M, 41, 48 TR&TL, 49 BR; Bell Bay Golf Club: p. 15 R; Inverary Resort (Cape Breton Resorts): p. 15 L; Cheryl Smith, OutFront Productions Inc.: p. 23; Les Trois Pignons: p. 28 T; G.B. Croft (Cape Breton Highlands National Park): pp. 32 B, 45 B; P. DeMone: 49 T; G. Heinze (Cape Breton Highlands National Park): 32 L; Stephen Homer (Cape Breton Highlands National Park): 31 T, 34; Destination Cape Breton (Cape Breton Highlands National Park): 35 B; H. MacLeod: 49 BL; G. Pleau (Cape Breton Highlands National Park): p. 37; Beaton Institute, University College of Cape Breton: 61 B, 66, 68; Highlands Links Golf Course (Milner Graphic Design): p. 49 B; Don Robinson: p. 73; Shutterstock: pp. 3, 18 T, 21, 33 BL, 35, 63 TR; Christian Newton: 20; Dennis Jarvis: pp. 47, 50, 71 T; Romane Souchko (Centre de la Mi-Carême): p 25 B

Formac Publishing Company Limited recognizes the support of the Province of Nova Scotia. We are pleased to work in partnership with the Department of Community, Culture, Tourism and Heritage to develop and promote our cultural resources for all Nova Scotians. We acknowledge the support of the Canada Council for the Arts.

Library and Archives Canada Cataloguing in Publication

Title: Touring the Cabot Trail and beyond / Susan Biagi ; photography by Keith Vaughan.
Names: Young de Biagi, Susan, 1957- author. | Vaughan, Keith, 1943- photographer.
Description: Fourth edition. | Includes bibliographical references and index.
Identifiers: Canadiana 20220493634 | ISBN 9781459507142 (softcover)
Subjects: LCSH: Cape Breton Island (N.S.)—History—Guidebooks. | LCSH: Cabot Trail (N.S.)—History—Guidebooks. | LCSH: Historic sites—Nova Scotia—Cape Breton Island—Guidebooks. | LCSH: Historic sites—Nova Scotia—Cabot Trail—Guidebooks. | LCGFT: Guidebooks.
Classification: LCC FC2343.2 .B53 2023 | DDC 971.6/91—dc23

cover photo: Shutterstock
cover designer: Tyler Cleroux

Formac Publishing Company Limited
5502 Atlantic Street
Halifax, Nova Scotia, Canada
B3H 1G4
www.formac.ca

Printed and bound in Canada.

CONTENTS

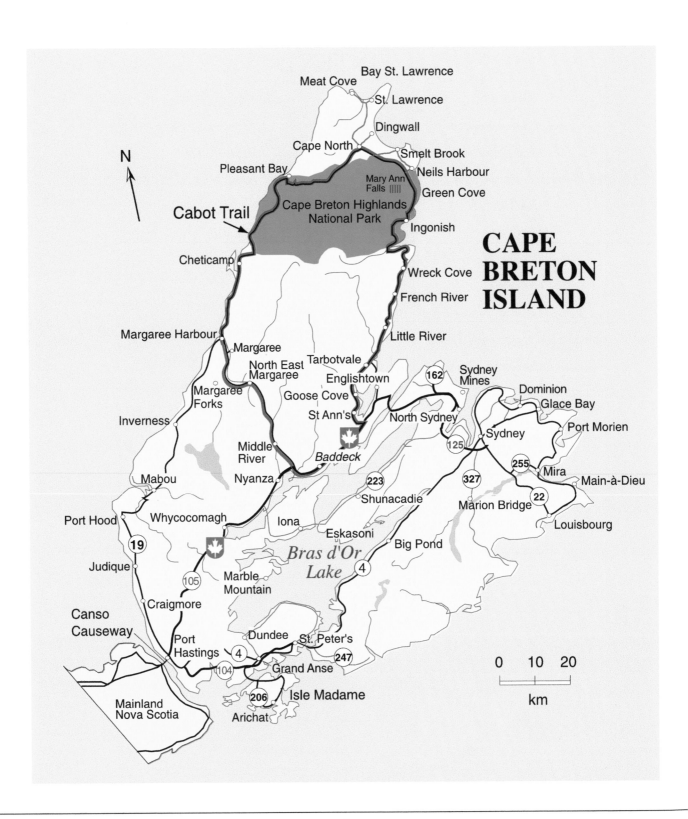

N

Bay St. Lawrence
Meat Cove
St. Lawrence
Dingwall
Cape North
Smelt Brook
Pleasant Bay
Neils Harbour
Mary Ann Falls
Green Cove
Cabot Trail
Cape Breton Highlands National Park
Ingonish
Cheticamp
Wreck Cove
French River
CAPE BRETON ISLAND
Margaree Harbour
Little River
Margaree
North East Margaree
Tarbotvale
Englishtown
162
Sydney Mines
Dominion
Glace Bay
Margaree Forks
Goose Cove
St Ann's
North Sydney
Sydney
Port Morien
Inverness
Middle River
Baddeck
125
327
255
Mira
Main-à-Dieu
Mabou
Nyanza
223
Shunacadie
Marion Bridge
22
Port Hood
Whycocomagh
Iona
Eskasoni
Big Pond
Louisbourg
19
Bras d'Or Lake
4
Judique
105
Marble Mountain
Craigmore
Canso Causeway
Dundee
St. Peter's
Port Hastings
4
247
104
Grand Anse
Mainland Nova Scotia
206
Isle Madame
Arichat

0   10   20
km

FOREWORD

For me, as for most Cape Bretoners, a tour of the Cabot Trail is a yearly pilgrimage. We usually make the trip in autumn, after the leaves have turned to red and gold. From Sydney, we leave before sunrise, shepherding sleepy and often grumpy children into the car. After digging out last year's mittens from the bottom of the closet, we set off, leaving behind the world of work, television, video games and answering machines.

From the back seat, inevitably, comes a drowsy warning, "Wake me up when we get to Kellys Mountain." According to legend, the mountain once belonged to an old Irishman, named Kelly, who lived there in somewhat inglorious solitude. At the summit of the mountain, a local artist has painted her conception of a red-haired and red-bearded Kelly. The two younger children wake, while even our teenaged son unplugs his iPod. We sit in silent tribute to a man who probably didn't exist but who is somehow part of who we are.

This is the time to weave the stories they won't always listen to when fully awake. Sometimes, it's inconvenient to have a historian for a mother. Children wrapped in thoughts of the future are not always interested in knowing that Canada's first lighthouse was built in Louisbourg. Or that the first west-to-east transatlantic wireless message was sent from Table Head, near Glace Bay. ("We know Mom, you told us that last year.")

But now, only half-awake, and caught in Kelly's spell, they listen to tales of the Mi'kmaw hero Kluskap, asleep under the sacred mountain. Looking up at the rugged line of hills, we try to trace the contours of his sleeping body. Maybe today is the day when he will arise and shake off his blanket of autumn leaves, to walk among his people once more.

By the time we reach Baddeck, everyone is bright-eyed and voluble, anxious to share their knowledge. The discussion turns to computers, with the children leading the way: "Do you know that Alexander Graham Bell was the grandfather of fibre-optics? And hydrofoils?" As the least technologically literate person in the car, I'm left to follow the conversation as best I can. Leaning back against the seat, I take delight, as my own parents did, in my children's discovery of the Cabot Trail.

From now on, I'm a willing (and somewhat smug) follower in this great adventure. Much of it is on foot. From the top of a seemingly vertical mountain, my two sons call down to me, "C'mon Mom, you can make it!" Satisfied of my safety, they turn away to savour the freedom of the high, windy plain. Our calls to them go unheeded and unheard, as they race across the top of the world. Below, my husband is still struggling to reach the summit, our daughter slung over his shoulder. I wonder: as an adult, will she be puzzled by dreams of moving, upside down, through a glorious land?

They will have to discover for themselves what it all means, this brilliant and diverse heritage. As they seek their own place in this wide world, their thoughts may turn to the Acadians, whose wanderings led them to a new home in Cape Breton. As the weather continues to change, they may look to the Paleo-Indians, who survived similar climatic upheavals. And, always, there is the example of Alexander Graham Bell, whose determination to achieve the impossible resulted in the invention of the telephone. All this belongs to them, just as it belongs to you.

— Susan Biagi

CANSO CAUSEWAY

The Canso Causeway

The difference is apparent as soon as the island comes into view, a mass of black hills rising beyond the Strait of Canso. Cape Bretoners can never see those hills without hearing music, a hum just below the level of ordinary consciousness. Before you know it, you'll be doing it too.

The island of Cape Breton is linked to the mainland by the Canso Causeway, constructed in 1955. At 65 m (213 ft), this is the deepest causeway in the world. Located on the great circle shipping route, the Canso Strait welcomes some of the largest ships and drilling rigs. Vessel traffic has the

Between Mabou and Inverness

Church in Inverness

West Mabou

the lowlands, spring usually arrives in early May, unlike the highlands where snow may persist until mid-June. Campers are advised to pack plenty of warm clothing, bedding and hot drinks. It is not unusual to awake and find water frozen in the cup.

Once across the strait, all traffic is funnelled to the rotary in Port Hastings. From here, there are several choices. Cape Breton boasts a number of scenic highways, including the Cabot Trail, the Fleur-de-lis Trail, the Marconi Trail and the Ceilidh Trail. All of these trails and many of the communities that lie along them will be described later. Both the Fleur-de-lis Trail and the Marconi Trail can be reached by proceeding east from Port Hastings.

To the west, the Ceilidh Trail winds through the communities of Troy, Creignish, Judique, Port Hood, Mabou and Inverness. The Gaelic word "Ceilidh" (KAY-lee) means "party" or "visit," usually held in the kitchen to the strains of fiddle and piano. This is the country that nourished ancient Celtic music, then gave it back to the world. Fiddler Natalie MacMaster hails from the tiny community of Troy, while the village of Mabou has given us John Allan Cameron and the Rankin Family, as well as Rita and Mary Rankin. And of course, Buddy MacMaster, one of the world's top traditional Scottish fiddlers.

Mabou comes later in this book. From the causeway, this "tour" takes the Trans-Canada Highway (Route 105) towards Baddeck, stopping first at Whycocomagh.

right of way. On the Cape Breton side of the causeway, a swing bridge allows small vessels to pass from the Gulf of St. Lawrence into the Atlantic Ocean.

Both bodies of water exert a moderating influence on the weather, resulting in pleasantly warm summers and mild winters. Being shallower and less salty than the Atlantic, the Gulf of St. Lawrence has slightly warmer water temperatures. On the island's west coast, water temperatures reach 18°C (64°F), as opposed to the cooler Atlantic temperature of 15°C (59°F).

On land, summer temperatures range from 20 to 25°C (68-77°F) in the daytime, while winter temperatures vary between -10 and 5°C (14-41°F). Altitude and relief have far more impact on island temperatures than latitude. In

THE ROAD TO BADDECK

Although English is spoken everywhere, the sounds of Gaelic, Acadian French and Mi'kmaw also resonate throughout the island. Two communities, one Mi'kmaw and the other Scottish, are situated at the extreme end of St. Patrick's Channel, at the head of the Bras d'Or Lakes. (The word Mi'kmaq refers to the people themselves, while the language is known as Mi'kmaw. The word Mi'kmaw is also used as an adjective.)

The Scottish community of Whycocomagh (Why-COG-o-mah) was established in 1821,

Near Whycocomagh

by Highland Scots. It takes its name from the Mi'kmaw word "We'koqma'q," which means "Head of the Waters."

Adjacent to Whycocomagh, the Mi'kmaw reserve of We'koqma'q has an even longer history. Traditionally, this entire area was part of the ancient hunting and fishing grounds of the Mi'kmaq, an Algonquian people with linguistic ties to the Maliseet of New Brunswick and the Innu of Labrador. Linguists believe that all Algonquian languages descended from an earlier, ancestral language known today as Proto-Algonquian.

Most First Nations east of the Rockies and down along the Atlantic seaboard speak an Algonquian language. The Iroquois are an important exception. Advancing from the south, into modern-day Ontario and Quebec, the Iroquois drove a wedge between the various groups of Algonquian peoples. For centuries, the Iroquois-speaking Mohawk were the traditional enemies of the Mi'kmaq. Finally, in the eighteenth century, the two peoples established a lasting peace that endures to this day.

Traditionally, the Mi'kmaw nation stretched from Gaspé in the north, to New Brunswick's St. John River in the south. It also encompassed all of modern-day Nova Scotia and Prince Edward Island, as well as parts of Newfoundland. Highly mobile hunter gatherers, the Mi'kmaq selectively exploited a variety of habitats. In summer, they gathered in large groups on the coast, to harvest shellfish, lobster and cod. A sophisticated harpoon technology and superb skills in seamanship were used to pursue the whales that abounded offshore.

By winter, the Mi'kmaq split into smaller, family groups,

moving deep into the woods to pursue the caribou, deer and moose that also sought refuge there. The territory of each family was determined by the natural carrying capacity of the land. Among the Mi'kmaq, each family tract averaged approximately 322 sq km (200 sq mi) of territory. The peo-

Negemow Basket Shop mural, Whycocomagh

ple spent the winter hunting and trapping. In spring they built weirs to catch the Atlantic salmon that came upriver to spawn. Standing in the still-icy waters of the river, they speared the enormous fish that return each year to their place of birth in an unceasing cycle of migration.

Contact between Europeans and First Nations was established sometime in the early sixteenth century. From that time on, the Mi'kmaw seasonal migration to the coast coincided with the annual arrival of fishermen from Europe. With the fishermen quick to recognize the market value of the Mi'kmaw furs, a flourishing trade was soon established between the two groups. Each year, when the Mi'kmaq vacated the inland forests, they loaded their canoes with exquisite pelts of beaver and moose. These were brought to the ships that waited in coastal harbours.

At first the fishermen posed little threat to the Mi'kmaw lifestyle. With the fishermen confined to the cobblestone beaches, near the fishing grounds, there was ample shoreline for everyone. For centuries the fisheries remained a seasonal industry, with most fishermen returning to Europe in the fall. Only one-third of the fishermen based at Fortress Louisbourg chose to spend the winter in North America.

This situation changed in the 1760s, when the region was awarded to the British. Soon after, in 1784, hundreds of refugees from the American Revolution sought refuge in Cape Breton. They were later joined by Scottish and Irish settlers fleeing famine in Europe. In the first half of the nineteenth century, over 20,000 Scots arrived in Cape Breton.

They arrived to a government in chaos. Lacking both surveyors and funds the tiny colonial government was hamstrung, unable to provide the newcomers with either land or supplies. Finding that no land had been set apart for them, many refugees simply squatted on crown land. They were prepared to defend their new farms at gunpoint.

This was a period of great suffering for everyone involved. As the land filled with settlers, the Mi'kmaq found their traditional routes from forest to ocean blocked. To earn a living, some turned to farming, others to fishing. Still others formed a market economy, selling baskets and other items to the coal towns springing up on the island. With the development of the sport fishery in Margaree, Mi'kmaw men became guides to American sport fishermen.

Even in the face of these enormous challenges, the Mi'kmaw nation survived, finding strength in its language, culture and family life. On Cape Breton Island, there are currently five Mi'kmaw reserves, known as We'koqma'q, Wagmatcook, Eskasoni, Chapel Island and Membertou. Today, through the media of poetry, literature and music, the Mi'kmaq are sharing their culture with the larger world. Elders teach the old ways to Mi'kmaw schoolchildren. The future of their nation is in excellent hands.

Chapel Island

HIGHLAND VILLAGE, IONA

In Cape Breton, your route depends on your state of mind. From Whycocomagh, the Trans-Canada Highway heads immediately for Baddeck, the traditional beginning and end of the Cabot Trail. Those who wish to begin their odyssey in a more leisurely fashion, however, should take exit 6 to Little Narrows, where the highway ends abruptly at a ferry wharf. No matter how hurried your state of mind, the ferry will slow you down, giving you time to study the horizon and reflect on the wake.

In many ways, this journey is a slow voyage into the past. Up ahead, at Iona, the Nova Scotia Highland Village is a time capsule of the early nineteenth to the early twentieth centuries. Situated on 17 ha (43 acres) of meadowland, the village is made up of 11 historic buildings from the island's Scottish past. Some were floated here on barges from communities located all around the lakes. Others were constructed as replicas of old houses that did not stand the test of time or prosperity. The Hebridean-style blackhouse is a replica of the houses left behind in Scotland. For centuries, Scottish Highlanders had lived in these small

Highland Village

Inside forge at Highland Village

huts, with only a stone wall to separate them from their animals. Smoke from peat fires wafted out through spaces in the thatched or turfed roofs. Upon their arrival in North America, the settlers built their own versions of these traditional houses. Later, they built sturdy woodframe houses made with the abundant supply of lumber.

In addition to houses and barns, the Highland Village also has a working forge, a schoolhouse, a carding mill and a store. A recent addition, the very old Malagawatch Church was moved on a floating barge down Bras d'Or Lake to the village. A wagon donated by the family of Alexander Graham Bell is also on display. Throughout the summer, there are demonstrations of butter-making, weaving and quilting. For those who are anxious to discover their Scottish roots, the Roots Cape Breton Genealogy and Family History Centre offers a computerized genealogical research service.

The museum is open daily, with full services extending from early June to the end of the Celtic Colours Festival in October. Highland Village Day is held on the first Saturday of August. Seated on the wide, grassy meadow, visitors enjoy Scottish concerts, square dances and other traditional activities. Few things can compare with the view from a

Cape Breton hillside in August, with the brilliant blue of sky and lake in the distance. Just below, children dressed in distinctive clan tartans trip lightly through traditional dances. In September, Pioneer Day gives visitors a chance to participate in soap-making, candle-making, fireplace cooking and other traditional activities.

Across the Barra Strait from Iona lies the community of Grand Narrows. It was here, in 1847, that the MacNeil Brothers, Donald and Sandy Hector, established their ferry service. Passengers were rowed across in a flat-bottomed scow, while horses and cattle swam alongside.

Times change. Even in the rural tranquility of Cape Breton, progress is inevitable. By the 1880s, cows were being herded across a brand new rail bridge. In 1923, the scow was replaced by a one-car ferry, run by a 14-horsepower motor. The first car to cross the Barra Strait was a Studebaker, from Sydney. The present bridge was opened in 1993.

Black House, Highland Village exterior (above); interior (left)

From Grand Narrows, it is a short drive to Christmas Island, where early birds can have their Christmas cards stamped with the Christmas Island postmark! From here, route 223 continues on to industrial Cape Breton. The route back across bridge and ferry, however, leads to Baddeck and the Cabot Trail.

BADDECK

From Little Narrows the Trans-Canada proceeds northeast to Baddeck, traditionally considered to be both the beginning and end of the Cabot Trail. Originally part of the hunting territory of the Mi'kmaq, Baddeck was later settled by Loyalists who were fleeing the American Revolution. For the next century it remained a peaceful farming village. Then, in 1885, there burst upon it an energetic, bristly haired, eccentric "pied piper" by the name of Alexander Graham Bell. Baddeck has never been quite the same since.

Bell was initially drawn to Baddeck by a travelogue, engagingly written in 1874 by Charles Warner, and entitled *Baddeck and that Sort of Thing*. Captivated by the scenery, which reminded him of his native Scotland, Bell wasted

Bras d'Or Lake

Alexander Graham Bell (above)
The Bell Museum, Baddeck (right)

Robert Baldwin. As an engineering student at the University of Toronto, Casey Baldwin seemed destined by breeding and education to play a key role in the history of central Canada. Fate intervened however. Baldwin came to spend a single summer with Bell in the highlands of Cape Breton and stayed for a lifetime. In addition to helping Bell with his experiments, Baldwin also spent a term as a member of Parliament, representing the farmers of Victoria County. His political legacy is Cape Breton Highlands National Park.

no time in settling in. Before long the people of Baddeck were being pulled, willy-nilly, into his experiments. In his workshop on the hill, young girls patiently sewed hundreds of red silk cells used to construct giant kites. Bemused farmers were given tours of the luxurious "Sheepsville," a model farm housing Bell's experiments in genetics. A gardener recruited to hold the kite ropes found himself suddenly borne aloft, dangling thirty feet above the crowd. Townspeople turned out in droves to witness the first flight in the British Empire, or see the fastest watercraft in the world, skimming like a dragonfly across Baddeck Bay.

In his work, Bell was helped by a quartet of young men, each of whom would win immortality through his association with the famous inventor. Thomas Selfridge, of the United States, went on to fly with Orville Wright, and later became the first airplane fatality. Glenn Curtiss, who began building engines for Bell's kites and airplanes, became one of the great names in the history of American aviation.

Two of the group were Canadian born. Frederick "Casey" Baldwin was the grandson of Canadian statesman

Unlike Casey Baldwin, J.A.D. (Douglas) McCurdy was born in Baddeck, the son of Bell's private secretary. His mother having died when he was a young boy, Douglas was often left to his own devices. His was a madcap childhood, spent wrestling with sails on the Bras d'Or Lakes and chasing kites on the hillside of Beinn Bhreagh. Mabel Bell was drawn to the motherless little boy, while her husband found him a ready helper. In time, Douglas's exuberant nature and devil-may-care approach to life made him the perfect aviator. In the days when airplanes were fragile contraptions of canvas and light wood, sheer bravado was one of the most desirable qualities in a pilot. On February 9, 1909, with the whole village of Baddeck on the ice to cheer him on, J.A.D. McCurdy flew into history as the pilot of the Silver Dart.

Alexander Graham Bell's work continues to be relevant

At the pier in Baddeck (above)
The Bell Museum (right)

with a complete replica. Built in 1918, this cigar-shaped vessel was the fastest watercraft of its time.

Situated on 4 ha (10 acres) of landscaped grounds, the Alexander Graham Bell National Historic Site also affords a fine view of Baddeck Bay. Bell's summer home, Beinn Bhreagh (ben VREE-ah, meaning "Beautiful Mountain"), is just visible across the water. The site is also kid-friendly. Special programs during the months of July and August introduce children to the joys of kite-building and kite-flying. Bell, whose two great loves were kites and children, would be proud of his legacy.

From the Alexander Graham Bell National Historic Site, it is just a short walk to the village centre. On the waterfront, the Bras d'Or Yacht Club maintains its place at the centre of village life. It too has a long and distinguished history. Casey Baldwin was one of its early commodores, while Mabel Bell established the Gardiner Hubbard Bell Challenge Cup. The Bras d'Or Yacht Club annual regatta, established in 1904,

today. His photophone, which successfully achieved optic transmission of sound, worked on the same principles as today's fibre-optic technology. Bell also experimented with binary systems, similar to those used in modern computers. He dreamt of solar heating panels and the production of methane gas from yard waste.

The Alexander Graham Bell National Historic Site is located at the east end of the village, on Chebucto Street. Full services extend from May through October, while reduced services are available throughout the year. All exhibits are fully wheelchair-accessible. One of the museum's most fascinating features is the collection of over 600 giant-sized photographs. Many of these were taken by Gilbert Grosvenor, Bell's son-in-law and former editor of the National Geographic magazine.

Other exhibits explore the chronology of Bell's life, from the telephone to the hydrofoil. Visitors can even listen to a recording of Thomas Watson's voice, recalling the famous transmission, "Mr. Watson — come here — I want to see you." The site's Hydrofoil Hall contains the original hull of the HD-4, together

Beinn Bhreagh

is still held each August. From the marina, visitors can take a free shuttle to the supervised beach on Kidston Island. (The name "Baddeck" is said to have come from the Mi'kmaw word abadeck, meaning "an island nearby.")

Baddeck's Inverary Resort was built in 1850, visitors can rent pontoon boats, kayaks, paddle boards, jet skis and more. Rest for a night in a lakeside cottage before teeing off at one of Baddeck's two golf courses. The Bell Bay Golf Club, located in the village of Baddeck, is an eighteen-hole course designed by Thomas McBroom. The Baddeck Forks Golf Club is a nine-hole course, off exit 9. From here, follow the signs to the provincial picnic park at Uisge Ban Falls (ISH-ga Ban, meaning "white waters," the standard Gaelic term for "waterfall"). The 15 m (50 ft) falls are situated at the end of a 7 km (4 mi) return hiking trail. An easy walk through a hardwood forest, this trail appeals to all ages, including very young children.

The Bell Bay Golf Club (above)
The Inverary Resort (left)

MIDDLE RIVER, LAKE O'LAW AND MARGAREE

Middle River

From the Trans-Canada Highway, exit 7 north to Hunters Mountain and the Middle River area marks the start of the Cabot Trail, which encompasses 298 km (186 mi) of highway, a variety of habitats, seven provincial parks, innumerable beaches and a plethora of waterfalls.

The land along the Middle River was settled by Highland Scots. Emigration from Europe began around 1815, when the end of the Napoleonic wars finally made it possible for people to leave. Freed from the armies and factories of Europe, thousands of Scottish and Irish emigrants set sail for North America, drawn by the abundance of land. The early arrivals received the best parcels, in river

valleys such as this one. Having chosen to leave by their own accord, they usually brought with them a little capital and some supplies. Those travelling with grown children were in the best position to take advantage of their new situation. With many hands to help on the farm, they soon prospered.

Later immigrants were not so advantageously placed. The enclosure movement in Britain had removed thousands of people from the land, to make room for sheep. So many of these came to Cape Breton that Nova Scotia author Thomas Haliburton called the colony "a refuge for the poor." Finding the good riverfront lands occupied, later arrivals settled on backland farms. Today, anyone travelling along the back roads of Cape Breton Island can still see the remains of these early farms. With land unfit for agriculture, many of these settlers survived by selling timber, or by augmenting their income with a little fishing or sheep farming. Others hired themselves out as labourers on better farms.

Picnic at Middle River

Margaree Valley

Most of the Scottish immigrants came from northwest Argyle, western Inverness-shire, Wester Ross and the Hebrides. By 1845, over 20,000 Scots had migrated to Cape Breton. By the 1870s, people of Scottish descent formed almost two-thirds of the island's population, changing its culture forever. Even now, their influence is so pervasive that most Cape Bretoners, no matter what their descent, speak with a distinctly Gaelic lilt.

As you proceed along this pleasant river valley, take some time to relax at the Lake O'Law Provincial Park, at the foot of the Three Sisters Mountain. From here the road continues on through the fertile Margaree Valley. The name Margaree is thought to come from the French "St. Marguerite." Scottish farmers lucky enough to settle in this area soon prospered. Situated almost halfway between Halifax and St. John's, Newfoundland, the farms were able to supply meat, milk, butter and cheese to these urban centres. Sheep farming, for wool and meat, was also important.

Salmon fishing also became a major industry in the area. Long considered as one of the finest fishing sites in the world, the Margaree River System has over thirty salmon pools, with names like Skye Lodge Pool, Chance Pool and Boar's Back Pool. The best fly-fishing occurs from mid-June to mid-July, and from September to mid-October. Licenses are available from local vendors.

Almost 130 km (80 mi) long, the Margaree system consists of two principal tributaries. The Northeast Margaree River flows from the Cape Breton Highlands in the north, while the Southwest Margaree River originates in Lake Ainslie, to the south. These two tributaries meet at

Fishing on the Margaree River

Margaree Forks, forming the Margaree River. From there the waters flow to Margaree Harbour, where they empty into the Gulf of St. Lawrence.

Because the water flows over granite rock, the riverbed is silt-free, providing the perfect habitat for Atlantic salmon. It is so perfect, in fact, that the Margaree has been designated a Canadian Heritage River. At Northeast Margaree, the Margaree Salmon Museum explores the impact that the river has had on Cape Breton's history.

Sponsored by the Margaree Anglers' Association, the museum contains exhibits of old fishing rods and tackle, including fly-tying techniques. There are even artifacts of the poacher's craft!

Salmon fry

Visitors can also tour the salmon hatchery on Hatchery Road. Located on a spawning stream, the hatchery intercepts adult salmon returning to their place of birth. Once the eggs are removed, fertilized and hatched, the juvenile fish are returned to the stream. Such hatcheries help ensure a high survival rate among salmonids.

Fishing is not all the area has to offer. At Margaree Forks, there is a nine-hole golf course. From Margaree Forks, a pleasant drive along the river, where cows graze in meadows along the river banks, leads eventually to Margaree Harbour, where a bridge crosses the river to Belle Côte.

To get to the actual community of Margaree Harbour, where there is an excellent beach, take a left turn off the Cabot Trail onto route 219 just before the bridge and drive a short distance to the Margaree Harbour Road.

Across the river at Belle Côte, back on the Cabot Trail, a left turn at the gas station leads to another fine beach and, in season, the opportunity to buy fresh lobster and crab.

INVERNESS AND MABOU

Broad Cove

By leaving the Cabot Trail temporarily at Margaree Harbour bridge, travellers can take time to explore the Ceilidh Trail (route 19). Turn off the Cabot Trail onto route 219 just before the bridge, and follow it southwest to Dunvegan. The Ceilidh Trail follows the western coastline of the island through Inverness, Mabou, Port Hood and many other communities, to Port Hastings.

Off route 19 at Dunvegan, on the Broad Cove Chapel Road, St. Margaret's Parish hosts one of the largest ceilidhs on the island. The first Annual Broad Cove Scottish Concert was held on August 7, 1957, in celebration of the parish church centennial. In rounding up the fiddling and step-dancing talent in the area, the organizers little dreamt that they were providing a training ground for the island's most promising young talent. Today, with the explosion in popularity of Celtic music, the concert attracts crowds numbering 8,000, no small achievement for a small, isolated parish.

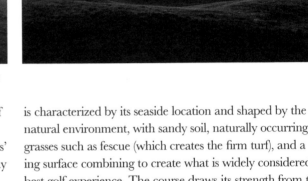

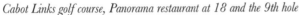

Cabot Links golf course, Panorama restaurant at 18 and the 9th hole

From Broad Cove the road continues on to the town of Inverness. Once a mining community, Inverness still possesses its distinctive company houses. The Inverness Miners' Museum, housed in the former Canadian National Railway Station, honours the town's coal mining past. These days, however, Inverness is better known as an increasingly popular tourist destination, complete with sandy beach and harness racing in the summer.

The beautiful Inverness County Centre for the Arts is open year round. Here there is a visual arts gallery and exhibition centre, as well as a small performance space, where local visual artists, artisans and performers are showcased.

A recent addition to the Inverness landscape is the Cabot Links Golf Resort. The site comprises a lodge with seventy-two rooms, nineteen villas, three restaurants and, not least, three golf courses, two rated in the World Top 100 by *Golf Digest*. Built atop the site of a former coal mine, the resort exhibits the changes that have taken place in the community, and has helped to restore hope for the future of Inverness. Bringing both employment opportunities and tourism to the area, the resort is a welcome addition to a town that continues to mourn the loss of its coal mining industry. Cabot Links opened in 2012, and the newer Cabot Cliffs officially opened in June 2016. Open seasonally from early May to early November, both are eighteen hole, true links courses — the only courses in Canada that can lay claim to that distinction.

A links course is the oldest style of golf course, developed in Scotland where the sport originated. This type of course is characterized by its seaside location and shaped by the natural environment, with sandy soil, naturally occurring grasses such as fescue (which creates the firm turf), and a rolling surface combining to create what is widely considered the best golf experience. The course draws its strength from the natural beauty this setting provides. Cabot Links is a walking course with caddies for hire and an ocean view for the full eighteen, and five holes directly on the shoreline, giving golfers ample opportunity to appreciate their surroundings here.

The brand new Cabot Cliffs course may well be even more spectacular. Before opening to the public, it was rated the Best New Course 2015 by *Golf Digest*, with suggestions that it might be a sincere rival to some of the all-time best courses like Pebble Beach and Cypress Point. Designed by the powerhouse team of Bill Coore and Ben Crenshaw, the course draws on the beauty of the cliffside coastline and challenges golfers to contend with the elements. The closing stretch, leading to the cliff's edge above the beach, is a joyous experience for anyone who truly loves the sport.

Of course, golf isn't the only experience the resort has to offer. The Cabot Links Lodge's seventy-two rooms all boast floor-to-ceiling windows with full views of the links. The nineteen oceanside villas, two bedroom and four bedroom, include a full kitchen, a private deck and an outdoor fireplace. The three on-site restaurants, Panorama, Cabot Bar and Cabot Public House, serve up a variety of dining experiences. Panorama's menu includes locally caught seafood, as well as pastas, game and fresh salads. Cabot Bar has a carefully considered wine list that includes both Canadian and international varieties, as well as a selection of whiskies.

Cabot Public House is the place to be for a more relaxed evening of music from local musicians, casual pub fare, including wood-fired pizzas, and local craft beers.

From Inverness it is a short drive to Glenville, home of the Glenora Inn and Distillery where Glen Breton Rare, Canada's first ever single malt whisky, is produced. The 365 ha (900 acres) site provides gorgeous views of rolling hills, and sits alongside the babbling MacLellan's Brook, which serves as the water supply for the distillery. Open seasonally from May to October, visitors can choose one of the nine rooms in the inn proper, or retreat to one of the six hillside chalets.

The scenic surroundings are part of what makes this highly rated whisky so special, and a true product of Cape Breton. Though every single malt whisky shares certain characteristics — being made from malted barley, from one distillery and aged at least three years — it is the confluence of environmental characteristics found only here that lend uniqueness to Glenora's offerings. The waters of MacLellan's Brook flow from nearby Mabou over tree roots and granite and marble. The surrounding forests, consisting mostly of maple and apple trees, with sprinklings of pine, spruce and cedar, lend their influence to the aging barrels in the warehouse. The temperate climate, not too cold in the winter and not too humid in the summer, allows for a

Glenora Distillery

Mabou Harbour lighthouse

gentle aging process. Taken together, these features create a whisky that couldn't be made anywhere else.

Start the day slowly, enjoying the view with a morning coffee, followed by a locally inspired lunch at the Washback Pub. The menu changes with the seasons, but you can count on both classic and innovative seafood dishes, designed by Chef Patrick MacIsaac. Follow this with a guided tour of the distillery, or, for the true whisky lover, make an appointment for the "Backstage Pass," which includes a private tutored whisky tasting and a sample drawn directly from the barrel. Visit the gift shop to take home a bottle of your own, or try it another way, with whisky cake and whisky fudge both on the menu.

Glenora's signature Glen Breton Rare came under fire in 2000 when the Scotch Whisky Association filed a lawsuit contesting the use of the word "Glen" in the name, claiming that this would lead international customers to believe the whisky was a product of Scotland. The trademarked name "Scotch" can only appear on whisky made in Scotland, where many of the world's mostly highly sought after whiskies are made. Though the Glen Breton name does have a distinctly Scottish ring, it's hard to argue that it doesn't simply illustrate the Scottish influence in Nova Scotia, where at least thirty-two communities contain "Glen" as part of their name. After a nine-year legal fight, Glenora won the right to continue use of the Glen Breton name. In 2010, Glenora marked this victory with the bottling of a special edition, fifteen-year-old Glen Breton fittingly titled Battle of the Glen.

Mabou is another short drive. This town was settled in the 1780s by Loyalists fleeing the American Revolution. It was not long, however, before the tiny population was inundated by the Scots who poured into the area.

There are many peaceful ways to spend an afternoon in Mabou. The Rail Trail, situated along an old railway line, is an excellent place to watch the bald eagles as they swoop down upon the fish glittering in the Mabou River. At the pioneer cemetery, old graves are sheltered by older trees.

For some, Mabou is a place of pilgrimage. The Mother of Sorrows Pioneer Shrine was built in the late 1920s, on the site of an early pioneer church. Although the exterior of this small white church is similar to many other churches in Cape Breton, its interior design is that of a miniature European cathedral. The Douglas Fir tongue-and-groove finish gives it a uniquely Canadian touch.

The shrine was restored in 1967 by the Brothers of Our Lady, who moved it 6 km (4 mi) to its present location. In 1989, ownership was transferred to the Episcopal Corporation of the Diocese of Antigonish. Today, its upkeep is derived from contributions from the Friends of the Shrine, as well as gift shop revenues.

Mabou is also home to Strathspey Place, a beautiful performing arts centre. Strathspey Place keeps locals and visitors entertained year round with concerts and ceilidhs featuring the talents of the many fine Inverness County musicians, as well as visiting performers.

Those who enjoy the exhilaration of a good hike have come to the right place. At West Mabou, along with a glorious beach, there is a network of well-groomed walking trails along the headland and through the adjacent woods. At Mabou Mines a spectacular system of trails criss-crosses the Cape Mabou Highlands all the way to Sight Point, just south of Inverness.

One excellent hike begins at the second bridge at the very end of the Mabou Mines Road. Take Fair Alistair's Mountain Trail (Beinn Alasdair Bhain), then follow the MacKinnon's Brook Trail to Sight Point.

Fair Alistair's Mountain Trail begins as a steady climb uphill along the coastline, and offers spectacular ocean views. Follow the trail down the other side to a gate and a dirt road. Follow the road for a short distance until you come to a fork. The road to the right circles the base of the mountain and leads back to your car. Save this road for when you are tired. It is a pleasant walk in the late afternoon, when the sun is slanting off the trees, and the sound of the brook is a soothing accompaniment.

Taking the road to the left, cross MacKinnon Brook

and follow the footpath that leads to the far mountains. After the second brook, the path divides again. The left-hand path leads down the river gorge to the ocean. The small beach is a fine place to eat lunch. The undertow here is strong and catches at the pebbles on the shore, but the high sides of the gorge form a small, protected meadow. In July, there are wild strawberries for dessert.

Retrace your steps, then follow the path that clings to the side of the mountains. From this height, you can see the outlines of the giant rocks that lie just below the surface of the water. The trail continues on through glens and across sudden drops and gorges. Below, a single hay field is under cultivation, recalling the days when these glens were populated. In the 1800s family groups landed on these beaches and claimed possession. Cape Mabou was settled by representatives of the MacInnis clan. Sight Point, at the end of the trail, was claimed by Alexander and Allan MacDonald in 1816. All are gone now. It may be, however, that the airs of ancient fiddles still keen in the wind.

In the highlands of Scotland, the fiddle was preceded by the "music of the mouth" and the "music of the body." Although not a native instrument, the fiddle was a natural successor to both, perfectly capturing the echoes and cadences of the Gaelic language. The melodies and arrangements also caught and preserved the spontaneous movement of the dancers as their feet rose and fell on the old wooden floors. The shuffling of the dancers' feet spiraled the music on to wilder and headier heights.

In Scotland, however, the music was silenced after the Battle of Culloden: the pipes and kilt were forbidden as they were deemed instruments of war. In the 1800s the clergy forbade the playing of the fiddles, going so far as to smash any found in the houses. Landlords laid violent hands on the people, throwing them off the land to make room for the sheep. Thousands of clansmen were lost to the industrial towns of Scotland's southern lowlands. Others died on the crossing to America. Many came to Cape Breton.

In Mabou, as in Scotland, the mountains rise directly from the sea, a familiar and comforting presence. From the glens of Scotland to the glens of Mabou, the people carried with them their language, their family loyalties and their music. Sheltered from the harsh world, the transplant took and thrived. Few had arrived with violins; instead,

The Celtic Colours Festival

they fashioned new ones from the spruce of their adopted country. Far from classical influences, the censure of the Scottish kirk and the fickle tastes of the dance halls, the music remained pure. Traditional arrangements and melodies were preserved and transmitted aurally, note for note, father to son, mother to daughter, as were the movements of the dance, as were the old Gaelic stories. Gaelic remained the language of the hearth, the farm and the church.

Today there is a flowering of Celtic music, as if it is finally time for the old ways to be shared. From the glens where they have been kept and preserved for almost 200 years, the old songs and stories are emerging. Fiddlers and arrangers, linguists and singers, poets and dancers travel throughout the world and welcome travellers in turn. Saturday night is still the time for the family square dance at West Mabou Hall, with all visitors welcome. And it isn't at all unusual for an internationally acclaimed musician, who just happens to be from the area, to drop by.

Seniors eagerly teach the steps to teenagers, who are just as eager to learn. From the glens, the ancient songs and stories pass into the hands of the whole world, for safekeeping. And when it comes to sharing Cape Breton's cultural heritage with the rest of the world, the annual Celtic Colours International Festival gets top billing. For an entire week early in October, Cape Breton vibrates with the non-stop strains of fiddles, bagpipes and Celtic guitars. In virtually every corner of the island, concerts and dances draw capacity crowds, and the after-hours ceilidhs carry the revelry long into the night.

CHETICAMP

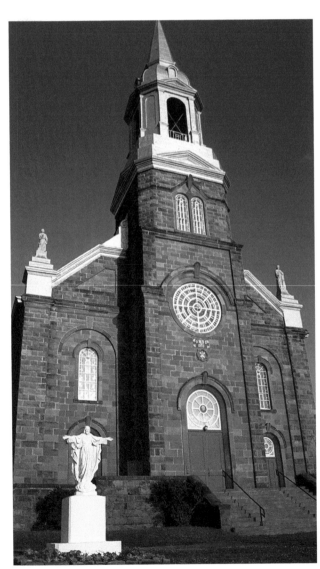

The Cabot Trail proceeds north along the coast from Margaree Harbour, through the Acadian communities of Belle Côte, Terre Noire and Cap Le Moine. Together yet apart, the Scots and Acadians have shared this region for over a century. Both groups began as refugees. The Scots fled famine, enclosures and political turmoil in Britain. The Acadians were deported from mainland Nova Scotia. In 1755, the British government made the decision to eject its French-speaking subjects from their communities along the shores of the Bay of Fundy. For the Acadians, this initiated a long, painful period of wandering. Some were shipped to the American colonies. Several hundred fled to French territory in Cape Breton and Prince Edward Island, only to be ousted again in 1758 after the fall of Louisbourg. From here, some went to Europe, others to French territory on the islands of St. Pierre and Miquelon. Although the Acadians were finally permitted to return to Nova Scotia

St. Peters Church, Cheticamp: above and right

A hooked rug at Les Trois Pignons, Cheticamp

The settlement of Cheticamp dates back to 1770, when French-speaking merchants from the English Channel island of Jersey established a summer fishing station in the area. The Acadians were recruited to settle here and fish for the Jerseymen. The first permanent residents arrived in 1785. For many, it meant a lifetime of credit, in debt to the company store. Yet many accepted, happy to return to their beloved Nova Scotia.

Although life was hard, they welcomed the isolation. In Cheticamp, the first settlers built their houses in the mountains, invisible to the British ships that patrolled the coast. As late as 1823, the road between the Scottish and Acadian communities remained a mere footpath. Here, in these isolated communities, the Acadians safeguarded their language and culture, their old songs and folk traditions. One of these was the holiday known as *la Chandeleur*. Dressed in bright rags, groups of young people would run from house to house, performing the old folk dance known as *l'escaouette* (les-coo-ETTE) and demanding food in return.

in 1764, their former lands on the Bay of Fundy were forbidden to them. Instead they settled on barren, rocky coasts, far from the centres of population.

At first, apart from the French road signs, there is little to indicate that you have passed into another realm. If you look closely, however, you'll see the distinctive sloped roofs on many of the older houses, a protection against the dreaded southeast gales that sweep down on the village from the mountains behind. Even in the face of 200 km/ hr (120 mi/hr) winds, these houses will not be swept away.

Look closer still and you'll see that most of these houses face the sea. Here and there a brightly painted fishing boat is mounted in the backyard. It wasn't always that way. On

Centre de la Mi-Carême, Cheticamp

the Bay of Fundy, before the deportation, the Acadians were farmers, famous for their fertile dyked meadows. Resettled on this coast, however, they became fishermen and shipbuilders.

On the road to Cheticamp, a colourful scene on the side of the road calls to mind this ancient tradition. At the Centre de la Mi-Carême whimsy and magic reigns as

Scenes of Cheticamp: above and left

a team of passionate guides tell you about the Acadian tradition. Participate in the frequent workshops, or explore the masks and local artisan goods.

Long before you reach Cheticamp proper, you can see the spire of St. Peter's Church. Built in 1893 with stone from Cheticamp Island, it too looks to the sea. From here, many prayers arose for the safety of the men fishing in small boats, or hunting seal on the ice in spring. In the quiet beauty of their church, one of the

Petit Etang

Rug-making at Les Trois Pignons

kitchen or family room. Family life going on all around her, the mother or grandmother sat contentedly hooking, each completed strand a promise of warmth over the coming winter. Like their clothes, the rugs were decorated with bright splashes of colour.

By the 1920s the distinctive rugs of Cheticamp had evolved into a cottage industry, with a cooperative established to market the product. Cheticamp native Elizabeth LeFort took rug-making to yet another level. Beginning at the age of twelve, LeFort began to create tapestries that now hang in the Vatican, Buckingham Palace, the White House and the National Museum of Civilization in Ottawa. Twenty of these tapestries can be seen at the cultural and genealogical centre known as Les Trois Pignons (The Three Gables). Other tapestries, produced by the women of Cheticamp, can be purchased in the centre's gift shop. Today the rugs are made from hand-dyed yarn. Cheticamp also offers saltwater bathing at the Plage St-Pierre (St. Peter's Beach), where the water reaches a warm 18°C (64°F) or more in summer. Nearby, Le Portage Golf Club offers a

most exquisite in Canada, the people have found some solace from the hardships of life.

Strength of faith was one of the most important factors in living here, along with resourcefulness. Little was wasted. Rags and old remnants of clothing were torn to pieces, to be hooked into rugs. The rug frame was often set up in the

Boats moored in Cheticamp

full, eighteen-hole course. Set against a backdrop of mountains, the clubhouse's 360° deck provides panoramic views of both forest and ocean.

Marine Life

In the village of Cheticamp, the waterfront's Le Quai Mathieu is a centre of village life. From here, small fishing boats leave regularly in search of the "catch of the day" for local restaurants.

Whale watching in Cheticamp

Whale-watching cruises can also be chartered from the quay. Located on the Gulf of St. Lawrence, Cheticamp lies on the migration routes of fin, minke and pilot whales. The fin whale is one of the world's largest animals, with some specimens attaining lengths of almost 26 m (85 ft). It is also the fastest of all the whales, gliding effortlessly through the water and occasionally leaping above its surface. At 6–9 m (20–30 ft) the minke holds its own beside its larger relative. Also a fast swimmer, the minke can travel at a speed of 24–30 knots. Not known for its shyness, it can suddenly appear alongside the boat, providing occupants with a wonderful surprise.

Both the fin and the minke whales are non-toothed whales, feeding benignly on zooplankton and small fish such as capelin and herring. Sometimes seen swimming on their side, mouth open, these whales sieve millions of minute crustaceans through their baleen plates. Their more ferocious companion, the pilot whale (known locally as the blackfish or the pothead), seeks larger prey such as cod, squid or mackerel. A toothed whale, it travels in family pods ranging from 10 to 100 animals.

Deep-sea fishing is also available in Cheticamp, with boatowners providing tackle. For families, one of the most popular activities is jigging for cod. Mackerel are caught with lures, mackerel flies and baited hooks. Travelling in schools, their streamlined bodies achieve great speeds. Greenish blue-black, with dark wavy bands on top and a silvery underbelly, the mackerel is a beautiful fish to see in the water.

Serious sport fishers should inquire locally about the possibility of giant bluefin tuna. Although this fish is more commonly caught in the Port Hood area, some commercial vessels in Cheticamp hold current licenses. These fish migrate to the Gulf of St. Lawrence in June and July, having spent the winter in the warm waters of the Gulf of Mexico. Good fighting fish, they must be caught by rod and reel on a licensed commercial vessel.

Lurking just below the surface of the water, the mako shark is another popular sport fish. Like the bluefin tuna, it too requires a federal fishing license. Great caution must be exercised in removing the shark from the line.

Just north of Cheticamp the Cabot Trail enters Cape Breton Highlands National Park.

CAPE BRETON HIGHLANDS NATIONAL PARK

Cabot Trail at Presqu'île

Canada has more than forty national parks and five national marine parks. Cape Breton Highlands National Park encompasses 950 sq km (365 sq mi) of wilderness, as well as some of the most scenic sections of the Cabot Trail. The northern portion of the Cabot Trail weaves in and out of the park, exploring scenic points and villages outside park boundaries. Food and lodging, are available every 30 km (19 mi), on average, with gas stations being much less frequent.

From the park's west gate in Cheticamp, to its east gate in Ingonish, total driving distance is 106 km (66 mi). Driving time is anywhere from two hours to an entire summer. To fully explore all the park has to offer, park officials recommend a minimum stay of four days.

Cycle tours of the entire Cabot Trail are available from local operators, with prior arrangement. Most runs average just over 70 km (44 mi) per day. Experienced cyclists find the route challenging, but rewarding. As the park continues

Grande Falaise

its work on upgrading the Cabot Trail to provide a paved shoulder to cyclists. Spring and fall cycling tours are great choices to avoid peak traffic.

Within the national park, full services extend from late-May through to the end of the Celtic Colours Festival in October. During this period, a National Park Entry Permit is required to use any park facility, including washrooms, campgrounds and sightseeing on the Cabot Trail. Entry permits are available at the park gate kiosks and at the two visitor information centres, located near the park gates in Cheticamp and Ingonish. One-day, multi-day and seasonal passes are available, with discounts on stays of seven days or more, for entry and camping. Entry permits must be prominently displayed on the window of your vehicle. All major credit cards, Interac/debit cards, traveller's cheques and cash are accepted for payment.

Fishing licenses for trout and salmon are also available at the visitor information centres. Be sure to inquire about fly-fishing regulations in scheduled rivers.

The Cheticamp Visitor Information Centre is located approximately 4.8 km (3 mi) north of the village of Cheticamp. Its hours of operation are:

- 9 am to 5 pm in the spring and fall
- 8 am to 8 pm in July and August

Telephone inquiries and on-site customer service are available at the park offices.

At the visitor information centre, take time to view the orientation exhibit, register for night hikes, grab a coffee and let children play in the nearby playground. The bilingual staff will be happy to answer all your questions, while the bookstore sells a wide range of literature, including maps and field guides.

Having obtained the necessary entry permits and fishing licenses, anglers can immediately cast their lines in the Cheticamp River. Located a few minutes walk from the centre, beginning near the Cheticamp Campground, the *Trous de Saumons* Trail (9.5km/5.9mi return) follows the Cheticamp River upstream to a series of salmon pools. The first pool is located 3.6 km (2.25 mi) upstream. Salmon fishing in the park is catch-and-release fly fishing only, restricted to the Cheticamp River, and requires a national park salmon license. Specific regulations apply to both general and salmon fishing within the park, so be sure to pick up a copy when you purchase your licenses.

Salmon Pool Trail

Bald eagle

skunk and porcupine are as yet unknown in this region. Nor are there venomous snakes. The island's most common snake is the harmless garter snake.

For people's safety, and the safety of the animals around them, it is illegal to feed or disturb wildlife within a national park. (Collecting of any kind, including plants, butterflies, rocks and kindling, is also strictly forbidden.) This is the habitat of the black bear. While the probability of meeting a bear is low, you should exercise some caution, especially near berry patches or fresh droppings. Campers should store all food in vehicles, tightly covered containers, or storage lockers where provided and use bear-proof garbage cans for waste. Pets must be on a leash at all times, for their own safety and for that of the wildlife around them. Park staff recommend that photographers use a telephoto lens when photographing wildlife.

If you do meet a bear, give it a wide berth, leaving the animal an adequate escape route. Bears are unlikely to

As the largest protected wilderness area in the Maritime provinces, Cape Breton Highlands National Park is a haven for a number of rare or threatened species. The park provides a welcome refuge for the rock vole, the Gaspé shrew and the pygmy shrew. It is also one of the last refuges for the Canada lynx and pine marten in Nova Scotia.

As you drive or walk through the park, you may encounter moose, deer, fox, bald eagles and snowshoe hare. Throughout most of Cape Breton's history, the Canso Strait served as a natural migration barrier, limiting the number of land mammals to about forty. With the completion of the Canso Causeway in 1955, however, several new species, including the raccoon, coyote and bobcat migrated here. The

Tern with her young, Tern Rock

attack unless threatened or cornered. Never approach a bear cub, for you can be sure that the mother is not far away. If the bear does show signs of aggressive behaviour, do not turn your back on the animal, but walk slowly backwards, speaking softly all the while. Never climb a tree. Bears are excellent climbers.

One of the best ways to appreciate the park's wildlife is on foot. Twenty-six hiking trails, ranging from short walks to arduous climbs, explore a variety of habitats. The trail known as *Le Buttereau* begins in the parking lot at Presqu'île Beach, near the towering, granite rock face known as the Grande Falaise. Before beginning, consult the map posted at the start of the trail. Originally a footpath used by the region's Acadian settlers, *Le Buttereau* winds along cliffs and through valleys, emerging on the coast then delving back into the woods. With spruce needles cushioning the ground and a canopy of branches above, hikers are led deeper and deeper into the cool depths of the forest. Listen for the songbirds: there are fully eighteen species of warblers. The black-capped chickadee, the purple finch, the white-throated sparrow and the robin also add their voices to the chorus. This trail joins with the Chemin du Buttereau, to emerge near the entrance of the Cheticamp campground.

CAMPING AND BACKCOUNTRY HIKING

Cape Breton Highlands National Park has seven front country campgrounds, operating from mid-May to mid-October, with full service in July and August. Reservations are available for Cheticamp Mkwesaqtuk/Cap-Rouge, Broad Cove and Ingonish Beach campgrounds. All others are assigned on a first come, first served basis. Campers who stay for seven or more consecutive nights get a 15 per cent discount.

The campgrounds offer a variety of electrical and unserviced sites, as well as fully serviced sites. With the exception of the campground at Big Intervale, all campgrounds offer the convenience of flush toilets. Showers are available at the Cheticamp, Mkwesaqtuk/Cap-Rouge, Broad Cove and Ingonish Beach campgrounds. Many campgrounds also provide playgrounds and kitchen shelters, Emergency phones and shelters are located strategically on French, MacKenzie and North Mountains.

Campfires are restricted to the fireplaces provided. Firewood is sold locally or on-site by the bundle. Bring along an axe to make kindling. It is unlawful to collect kindling within the park.

Park staff present a variety of interpretative programs,

Fishing Cove

Acadian Trail

concentrating on the area's natural and human history, at interpretive venues in the major campgrounds. Night security is available throughout the months of July and August.

Wilderness camping is permitted at Fishing Cove with the purchase of a backcountry permit. Bring along a backpacking stove and boil all drinking water. All garbage must be packed out.

Winter Sports

In the highlands, altitude and prevailing continental winds bring long, cold winters, with annual snowfalls reaching as high as 400–500 cm (15–20 ft). Snowshoers and cross-country skiers can delight in a variety of ungroomed trails, and a silence that is almost absolute. North Highlands Nordic in Cape North has a scenic network of groomed trails for those seeking a less rugged experience.

South of the park, Cape Smokey offers downhill skiing with spectacular views of the ocean. Those who prefer to keep their centre of gravity a tad closer to the ground might consider tobogganing on the fifth fairway at the Highlands Links Golf Course.

Snowshoers in Cape Breton Highlands National Park

French and MacKenzie Mountains

MacKenzie River Valley

Leaving sea level, the road ascends French Mountain. Here, on the park's western coastline, Cap Rouge (Red Cape) is one of the most well-known scenic views in Canada. Geological faults have helped carve the highest mountains and the deepest valleys in Atlantic Canada. From here, the mountains rise to over 500 m (1700 ft). Rocks over a billion years old, among the oldest in Atlantic Canada, can be found here.

At its highest point the highway on French Mountain reaches elevations of 455 m (1492 ft). At the plateau, vegetation is predominantly Boreal-Taiga, with such arctic-alpine plants as whortleberry and dwarf birch. Higher on the plateau, reindeer lichen and sheep laurel cling to the exposed stone. The soil, what there is of it, is thin and sparse, with talus slopes. Trees are stunted, buffetted by the "Krummholz effect" of the wind and the scouring effect of the ice. Barely a metre in height, they have nonetheless won the struggle for survival. Some are 150 years old.

While ascending the mountain, look at the bare, rounded cliff far above the highway. It may be possible to discern human figures standing on the observation platform at the end of the Skyline Hiking Trail. To reach this trail, turn left at the top of the mountain, and follow the gravel road to the large parking area, where you will also find latrines. The trail is a relatively easy 8.2 km (5.1 mi) hike that leads to the spectacular Headland Cliff and loops back again to the beginning. Extensive work has been done on this scenic cliffside trail, to compensate for the heavy wear and tear it sustains from thousands of enthusiastic hikers each year. From the viewing decks watch for whales in the Gulf of St. Lawrence and bald eagles soaring overhead. This is a favourite spot for moose, as well as bear, and for that reason dogs are NOT permitted. Allow yourself 2 to 3 hours to truly enjoy this trail.

From Skyline, hikers can continue on to the Bog Trail, a wheelchair-accessible, 0.5 km (0.3 mi) loop of boardwalk. As the last ice age ended approximately fifteen thousand years ago, receding ice gouged out a series of depressions in the hard rock of the region. These depressions, in turn, became glacial ponds filled with water from the melting ice. Located high above the water table, with no source of replenishment, the lakes soon became clogged with sphagnum moss. Rushes and sedges began to grow in the wet sludge, while the carnivorous sundew, bladderwort and pitcher plants fed on insects. Look closely. At the top of the mountain there are orchids growing, a brilliant splash of colour in a brown world.

Here in this world of bogs and barrens, streams are born, tea-coloured from the tannic acid that leaches out of the peat. There are seventeen major watersheds and canyons within the park. The Cheticamp, MacKenzie and Grand Anse Rivers all empty into the Gulf of St. Lawrence, while the Black Brook, Clyburn and Aspy rivers flow towards the Atlantic.

Wildlife is hardy. This is the habitat of the moose, black bear, lynx and marten. Five thousand years ago, the ancestors of the Mi'kmaq hunted woodland caribou on this high, windy plateau. Later, both Mi'kmaq and Acadians depended on moose as a major food source. Throughout the early period of settlement, the moose was a far more common sight than most farm animals, so common that the Mi'kmaw word for "cow" is equivalent to "French moose."

The moose also provided the people with clothing. The Mi'kmaq taught the Acadians how to prepare the skins, first by smoking and then by massaging a special mixture of inner organs and oil into the hide. Among the Mi'kmaq, every part of the moose was used. The bones were made into tools and sewing needles. The sinew was made into fine, white thread, perfect for the delicate embroidery that decorated all Mi'kmaw garments.

Skyline of the Cabot Trail

Today, no hunting is permitted inside the national park, while hunting outside the park is strictly controlled, and moose populations carefully monitored. Both moose and woodland caribou disappeared from the island in the early 1900s, the victims of overhunting. Moose were reintroduced into Cape Breton Highlands National Park in 1947 and 1948, when 7 bulls and 11 cows were successfully imported from the Elk Island National Park, in Alberta. A similar attempt to restore caribou populations, made in 1968, was not successful.

Past the Bog Trail, on the highway, the Fishing Cove Trail descends 355 m (1165 ft) to a small, isolated cove. Once the site of a fishing village and factory, Fishing Cove is the park's only designated wilderness campsite. (Campsites must be reserved by purchasing a permit at the visitor information centres.)

The Fishing Cove Trail is a fairly arduous, 12 km (7.5 mi) return hike. From the cove, on a clear day, you can see the Magdalen Islands across the Gulf. At your feet, the ground is lush with crowberries and blueberries. In the old days, when the cove was filled with families, harvesting them was a job for the women and children. Carrying baskets and old pots, they fanned out over the hillsides, collecting the precious fruit that grew there.

By fall, jars of preserves lined the shelves of the cellars and storehouses, providing insurance against the future. It was not enough. In the end, fishing villages such as these were abandoned and their people scattered. Today, their history is known only to those who scan the old photographs, or walk the trails to the secret coves.

From French Mountain, the highway passes directly to the summit of MacKenzie Mountain, 372 m (1222 ft) at its highest point. It was here, in 1947, that a fire devastated 2,835 ha (7000 acre) of forest. From this tragedy, however, arose a rare opportunity to witness the growth of a new forest. Interpretive panels at three look-offs along the mountain highlight the wonders of this region.

(Drivers should use low gear while descending all the mountains in the park. This includes vehicles with automatic transmissions.)

PLEASANT BAY AND GRAND ANSE VALLEY

The village of Pleasant Bay lies at the bottom of MacKenzie Mountain, just outside Cape Breton Highlands National Park. A working fishing village, Pleasant Bay offers a number of services, including a variety store, giftshops, service station, restaurants, accommodations and whale-watching tours. Beyond the village, stretching as far as the eye can see, the mountains rise directly from the sea floor. This is one of the most beautiful wilderness areas in Cape Breton, accessible only by foot.

The Polletts Cove trail extends 8.5 km (5 mi), 19 km (10 mi) return up the coast, winding through abandoned fishing villages and hidden coves. The area is private property, so please make sure to leave the area as you found it. Before embarking on this trail, make sure that someone knows your approximate time of return, and can alert the proper authorities if you do not return within a reasonable time.

A more accessible trail is the MacIntosh Brook trail, located in the Grand Anse Valley. From the small campground,

Pleasant Bay

"It was late fall," he recalls. "We had to break the ice in the brook to wash our faces. We worked nine hours, from 7 am to 5 pm. It was pick-and-shovel work, and we went steady all day long, clearing up the rubble left by the blasting."

While the work was hard, the meals were plentiful. "We got $1.50 per day, plus our meals. We had porridge in the mornings, with hot biscuits and piles of bacon and eggs. Anything you wanted to eat, and plenty of it."

There were other joys. On Saturday nights the men walked down the mountain into Neils

Constructing the Cabot Trail (above); after completion (right)

Scene along Cabot Trail, Cape Breton, N.S.

this 1.7 km (1.1 mi) return trail follows the brook upstream through a hardwood forest to a waterfall.

Well into the twentieth century, these secret glens were known only to hunters and fishermen. In Pleasant Bay, mail still arrived from Cheticamp by dogsled. Potential for tourism was limited. The region's fresh air and seawater had always attracted a number of Americans (such as Alexander Graham Bell), however, it was a rare and committed tourist who would brave the journey of train, steamer, ferry, cart and footpath to the isolated hills of Cape Breton.

All this would change with the advent of the automobile. Well-graded roads could make even the most isolated areas accessible. Convinced of the area's ability to attract tourists, the government embarked on an ambitious plan to blast a road out of the hard rock. In 1932, crews of workmen began the long, hard job of creating the Cabot Trail.

At the time, Cape Breton was in deep economic depression and the creation of the Cabot Trail provided needed employment in the area.

Edward Squires was sixteen years old when he was called to work on the new highway. For some families, he says, there were more mealtimes than meals. In an attempt to alleviate the worst ravages of the depression, local councillors rounded up young men like Squires to work on the road being blasted out of the mountain.

Harbour. Square dances were held right on the bridge in Hungry Cove, to the music of fiddle and harmonica. "It didn't matter to us," says Squires, "we were as rough as the bridge!"

Edward Squires worked in the camps for several seasons. Soon after the road was completed, World War Two took its place as the region's primary employer. The young men and women were off to new adventures in Europe.

Though a significant achievement, this early road left much to be desired. For many years, it permitted traffic in just one direction at a time. Today, in Cape Breton, there are many seniors who still remember parking their cars precariously on the side of a cliff, as a car proceeding in the other direction inched by. On Cape Smokey, the steepest of the mountains, drivers called from a phone situated at the base of the mountain, to make sure there was no oncoming traffic. The Cabot Trail was not paved until 1957.

LONE SHIELING

From the Lone Shieling of the Misty Island
Mountains divide us and the waste of seas,
Yet still the blood is strong, the heart is Highland,
And we in dreams behold the Hebrides.

I n creating Cape Breton Highlands National Park in
1936, the Canadian government opened the area to
tourists. It also ensured that the area's flora and fauna
would be protected from encroachment by loggers and

farmers. Today, at the Lone Shieling, visitors can walk through a stand of sugar maple that is over 350 years old.

The Lone Shieling owes its existence to a

Big Intervale

By the Lone Shieling

Lone Shieling

professor named Donald Sutherland MacIntosh who
donated one hundred acres of land to the Government
of Nova Scotia in 1934. The donation was made on the
understanding that the Province would maintain a small
park and build a replica of the original Lone Shieling, a
shepherd's hut located on Scotland's Isle of Skye.

Like the original, the Lone Shieling is a place of quiet
refuge to travellers. An easy trail wends through a cool
forest of sugar maple, birch, beech and oak. This is a
magnificent forest to visit in autumn, when the mountains
are a sheer wall of colour. Take a moment to refresh
yourself with the birdsong and the sound of the brook.

At its highest point the highway on North Mountain
reaches an elevation of 445 m (1460 ft). Straddling the
line of the Aspy fault, it is a sheer wall of gneisses, schists
and granite, bordered by the softer sedimentary rocks of
the lowlands. All along the line of the fault, the abrupt
drop results in waterfalls and deep gorges. As you descend
into the Aspy Valley, a road to the right, just around the
turn past Big Intervale leads to the 15 m (50 ft) Beulach
Ban Falls.

From here, the Cabot Trail follows the line of the
Aspy River, to the village of Cape North, outside the
park. The North Highlands Community Museum's
archives and artifacts explore the contributions that both
Indigenous Peoples and early settlers made to the history
of the region. The museum also houses an extensive collection of genealogical records.

Beulach Ban Falls

CABOT'S LANDING PARK AND THE MONEY POINT TRAIL

At the village of Cape North, the road divides. While the Cabot Trail continues east, a second road veers to the north, to Cabot's Landing Provincial Park. Here, on this long sandy beach at the foot of Sugarloaf Mountain, a monument commemorates John Cabot's arrival in North America. Was this the beach on which John Cabot planted his cross in 1497, claiming the land for England? Over the centuries the location of his exact landing has been the subject of some controversy, with both Cape Breton and Newfoundland claiming the honour.

Swimmers at Cabot's Landing

Scholars have puzzled over the few contemporary references to Cabot's voyage. Cabot's own records of the *Matthew*'s voyage have disappeared. All that remains are second-hand descriptions, contained in letters written by shipping agents and on maps drawn after the explorer's death.

Historians are particularly stymied by the lack of information concerning Cabot's point of departure. Although built in Bristol, England, the *Matthew* did not sail west directly from its home port. With no way to measure longitude, ships were restricted to sailing along lines of latitude. Cabot planned to sail in a northern latitude to Asia, then "coast" southward to Japan. His most likely point of departure was therefore somewhere along the Irish coast. Without knowing for sure, however, it is difficult to determine his landfall.

From the letters, we know that, according to plan, Cabot set off westward and sighted land in the north. Distances vary: some informants claim that he sailed 700 leagues, others 400. Distance sailed may also have been affected by the Labrador Current, pushing Cabot towards more southerly latitudes. Based on this information, his landfall may have been anywhere from Labrador to Maine. The letter writers seem to concur that Cabot landed on the

Cabot Landing

Meat Cove (above); Meat Cove Lodge (below)

mainland. Afterwards, he apparently spent about a month cruising in the region. On the return voyage, he sighted two islands, but did not land. According to the author of one of the letters, most of the land was sighted after turning back.

The limited amount of information just raises more questions. Was the mainland really continental North America? Were the two islands really islands, or were they peninsulas? From the sea, Newfoundland's Avalon Peninsula gives every appearance of an island. Without answers to these questions, it is impossible to determine Cabot's landfall. This fine Cape Breton headland, its mountains visible far out to sea, seems as good a place as any.

From Cabot's Landing, the road continues on to Bay St. Lawrence. Its twin capes, one on each side of the bay, offer excellent opportunities for hiking. To the west, Cape St. Lawrence harbours the scenic village of Meat Cove, surely one of the loveliest coves in all Cape Breton. The hiking trail begins at the last house, near the campsite. Although an easy walk through secret coves and abandoned villages, this trail

should not be attempted without a reliable map. The entire area is criss-crossed by a number of logging roads which can lead the hiker astray. This is extremely dangerous, particularly if temperatures drop suddenly, as they often do in the highlands. Here, as in Polletts Cove, remember to leave word of your approximate time of arrival back in the village.

The eastern cape, known as Cape North, offers the extremely challenging Money Point Trail. The trail begins at the top of the mountain overlooking Bay St. Lawrence, on the road leading to the radio tower. Park near the caution sign, advising motorists against descending without a four-wheel drive. After a continuously steep descent, lasting almost an hour, the trail opens upon an amazing vista of coast, lighthouse and shipwreck. St. Pauls Island, once known as the graveyard of the Gulf, is just visible offshore. The island's lighthouse and lifesaving stations for shipwreck victims were built in 1837.

St. Margaret's Church,
Bay St. Lawrence

In summer at Money Point, horses are set free by their owners, to run wild in the short grasses. The mountains are a tangible presence, radiating both strength and peace. Breathe it in. You'll need plenty of both for the long climb back up the mountain.

SCENIC LOOP AND NEILS HARBOUR

From the village of Cape North (as opposed to the cape after which the village is named), the Cabot Trail continues eastward to the coast. Just past Cape North, a small scenic detour leads to the fishing village of Dingwall, located outside the national park. Farther along the Cabot Trail, at South Harbour, travellers can either continue overland, directly to the village of Neils Harbour, or leave the park to follow another scenic detour along the coast, through the communities of Smelt Brook, White Point and New Haven.

Neils Harbour was first occupied by Newfoundlanders of Irish and English descent who were engaged in the

Near Dingwall

New Haven

board these small, sturdy boats. The last, known as the *Aspy III*, made its final trip in 1964.

Since then, other changes have taken place. The 1992 moratorium on the cod fishery has made the future increasingly precarious. Nevertheless, the wharf remains the hottest place in town. Whale-watching voyages leave in pursuit of the titans swimming just offshore.

With cod increasingly rare on these shores, fishermen now chug out to the grounds in search of lobster or snow crab. In spite of the latest advances in technology, such as electronic fish-finders and precise navigational equipment, the fishery remains very much a family business. Husband and wife both pull in the traps and share the duties on board. Children learn early the independence that life on the sea brings with it.

seasonal fishery. Each spring, fishermen left their homes in Newfoundland to fish off these rich banks. Eventually they made a permanent move to the area, ferrying families and household goods across the Cabot Strait.

It was a time when every farmer fished and every fisherman owned a cow. Small, hardy gardens provided turnips and potatoes, peas and carrots. Coffee, sugar and flour were shipped in by boat, in hundredweight bags. By the 1880s, coastal steamships had established more regular links with the larger centre of North Sydney, bringing passengers and news of the outside world. Even cattle were shipped on

Just past Neils Harbour, the Cabot Trail once again enters Cape Breton Highlands National Park. Beyond lies the Black Brook Beach and day use area. From the parking lot, Jack Pine Trail proceeds in a 2.3 km (1.4 mi) loop through one of several stands of jack pine located in the area. This trail intersects with the Coastal Trail, then circles back to the parking lot.

Black Brook

Jack pine

GREEN COVE AND MARY ANN FALLS

At Green Cove, a rocky headland extending into the Atlantic Ocean provides the perfect nesting habitat for seabirds, now the sole occupants of this granitic outcrop.

In the days before gasoline engines, Green Cove was the site of a summer fishing station. Although exposed to the ravages of wind and waves, such stations were closer to the fishing grounds than the nearby village of Neils Harbour. Each morning, fishermen in small shallops rowed out to the fishing grounds, or hoisted a small sail. Offshore, they jigged cod using hand lines, then rowed back to temporary camps along the shore. When the weather turned stormy, the men ran their boats to the shelter of Neils Harbour.

The advent of the gasoline engine was a welcome innovation in the lives of these fishermen. Now, they could steam out to the grounds each morning and return to the safety of the harbour each night. Stations such as Green Cove were abandoned, left to the seals and seabirds.

Past Green Cove, offroad from the Cabot Trail, follow the gravel road to Warren Lake. The largest lake in the park, it offers excellent opportunities for swimming and canoeing. Until flooding in the fall of 2021 closed it, another gravel road led to the popular Mary Ann Falls, where swimmers and sunbathers enjoy the sounds and sights of falling water. This road will remain closed until repairs are complete.

Mary Ann Falls

INGONISH

Back on the Cabot Trail, southward through the park, the road proceeds to the community of Ingonish. Further on, just past park boundaries, lies the community of Ingonish Beach.

The Mi'kmaw name for this area is Geganisg, meaning "remarkable place." Archaeological evidence suggests that Ingonish Island was used as a quarry by Paleo-Indians, who lived in Atlantic Canada between nine and ten thousand years ago. At a time when hunters used spears tipped with stone points, the region conducted a busy trade in cherts, rhyolites, agates and crystal. Spearpoints made with stone from Ingonish Island have been found on Prince Edward Island, more than 100 km (65 mi) away.

The Ingonish area was equally profitable to European fishermen, who used it as a base for their summer fishery. Some historians even suggest that Basque and Portuguese fishermen may have preceded John Cabot to North America. Each spring they set out from their villages in Europe in search of the cod, whale and seal in the Gulf of St. Lawrence. The cod was laid out on the cobbled beaches to dry; whales were rendered for their oil, using great ovens that belched black smoke. Historians believe that European fishermen and Mi'kmaw hunters may have collaborated in the whale hunt. As masters of the sea, the Mi'kmaw would have offered their excellent skills as harpooners, accepting European iron in return. There is strong evidence that the two groups even evolved common trade languages, which were combinations of Mi'kmaw and Portuguese, or Mi'kmaw and Basque.

In time, the Basque and Portuguese ascendancy in the area waned. Both countries had lost ships and manpower to the Spanish Armada, in its doomed attack on England in 1588. Over the next two centuries, France and England would compete for control of the region's fisheries. With the establishment of Fortress Louisbourg in 1713, French fishing properties were stretched all along the island's northern and eastern coast, including Ingonish. All cod was shipped to Louisbourg, which served as the island's marketing centre.

With the fall of the fortress in 1758, both Acadians and French nationals were deported from the island. Although permitted to return in 1764, few settled in Ingonish. Instead, the area was peopled by Loyalists fleeing the American Revolution and Scots fleeing famine in Europe. They were joined, as we have seen, by Irish fishermen from Newfoundland. In those days, there was cod enough for all.

In the years that followed, people continued

Keltic Lodge

to be drawn by the region's natural resources, especially the long, sandy beaches, salt water and towering

Corson home (left); gates to Corson home (above)

mountains. Among the first to appreciate the region's beauty was an American couple, Henry Clay Corson and his wife, Julia Corson, who came to the area in the 1890s. At the time, Julia was suffering from tuberculosis. In the days before antibiotics, the usual cure was a prolonged dose of invigorating mountain air and salt water. Corson may have learned about Cape Breton from his friend, Alexander Graham Bell. As a boy, Bell's own father had regained his health in Newfoundland, and the family remained convinced of the area's health-giving benefits.

Whatever his initial impulse toward Cape Breton, Corson purchased land on the Middle Head peninsula for $120. Local legend has it that the couple spent their first summer in a wigwam. In spite of this unusual residence, or perhaps because of it, Julia completely recovered her health. The wigwam was soon replaced with an imposing home which would, in time, become the original Keltic Lodge.

Like the Bells, Henry and Julia Corson made every effort to fit into the community, purchasing cattle and housing them in a heated barn. As with Bell's "Sheepsville," this probably aroused some comment among local farmers whose own hardy cattle often sheltered on a wintery hillside.

The Nova Scotia government purchased the Corson home and property in 1938, two years after the establishment of Cape Breton Highlands National Park. The original Keltic Lodge was opened in 1940 in the old Corson

home. The older building was torn down when the present lodge was erected in 1951. Lying within the boundaries of Cape Breton Highlands National Park, it is owned by the Province of Nova Scotia and privately operated. Since its establishment, Keltic Lodge has received many prominent guests, including the Crown Prince of Japan.

Highland Links golf course

MIDDLE HEAD TRAIL

From the winding trail of birch at the entrance to the Keltic Lodge the grounds remain very much as they were during the Corsons' period of residence. The Middle Head trail begins at the parking lot of the Lodge and extends the length of the peninsula, to the ocean. Here, the unforgiving winds and waves have long since washed away the soft sedimentary stone, leaving a core of pure, hard granite that juts into the Atlantic.

Waves at Middle Head

About 4 km (2.5 mi) long, return, the Middle Head Trail begins in a small, protected wood, then opens out into a large meadow. Once a fishing village, the land is

returning to its original state. The small, hardy gardens so common to fishing communities have long ago succumbed to grass and cow vetch. In July, wild strawberries grow in profusion.

As you approach the ocean, the vegetation becomes increasingly twisted. Here, small spruce trees have been buffetted by the wind and the ocean spray. There they cling, determined to wrestle a blessing from the hard rock. Far off, to the right, Cape Smokey looms, steadfast and inexorable.

The birds are a surprise. A glance reveals that the whole rock teems with life. Throughout the summer, the community of seabirds is loudly and busily engaged in courtship rituals and child care. Perched on the sea stack, with black wings folded, the cormorants are tuned to the sub-surface flicker of a passing school of herring. The guillemot, black with a white patch on the wing, explores the rock crevices in search of the perfect nesting place.

Middle Head Trail (above and right)

Ingonish Beach and Area

In addition to the Keltic Lodge, the Ingonish area offers a variety of accommodations, including the Broad Cove and Ingonish Beach campgrounds, with a variety of serviced and unserviced sites, plus showers, kitchen shelters with wood stoves, and playgrounds. Ingonish Beach offers delicious saltwater and freshwater bathing, with lifeguards on duty during the months of July and August.

At the Highlands Links, near Middle Head, golfers will encounter one of the world's best courses. Its designer, Stanley Thompson, also created St. George's in Toronto, as well as the Banff and Jasper courses in Alberta. The Highlands Links is a public course, owned by Parks Canada and operated by Golf North. Services include an online tee booking system, power carts, and showers. Members can make use of on site lockers.

This is one of the few courses in the world where moose sightings are not unknown. Designed in 1939, in the Scottish tradition, this eighteen-hole course is located in the lush valley of the Clyburn River, within the boundaries of Cape Breton Highlands National Park. The first hole, known as Ben Franey, offers views of Franey Mountain. The eighteenth hole is known, appropriately, as "Hame Noo" (Scots for "Home Now").

Behind the golf course, the Clyburn Valley hiking trail (8.5 km / 5 mi return) leads to the ruins of a gold mine, established in 1911. Unhappily, although some of the ore was rich in gold, the veins soon ran out.

The Ingonish area also offers some of the best skiing in the province. Ski Cape Smokey is located outside Cape Breton Highlands National Park, at Ingonish Ferry. At 305 m (1000 ft), it is the highest ski hill in Nova Scotia and receives the most snowfall.

CAPE SMOKEY

From Ingonish Harbour and Ingonish Ferry, the highway rises abruptly to Cape Smokey, the most formidable of all the mountains. Named for the mist that often envelops it, Cape Smokey is 366 m (1200 ft) above sea level at its highest point. Although not the highest of the mountains, it is certainly the steepest, with its descent achieved in just 1.6 km (1 mi). On several of its hairpin turns, your car will seem suspended in mid-air, high above the Atlantic Ocean.

At the summit, Cape Smokey Provincial Park offers a bird's eye view of the world. The 10 km (6.2 mi) return hiking trail sets off through low shrubs, to emerge on sandstone cliffs. From here, there is a spectacular view of Middle Head and South Bay Ingonish.

From Cape Smokey, the road proceeds to Wreck Cove with its rocky shoreline that says everything about its name. Today, Wreck Cove is the site of the Nova Scotia Power Corporation's hydro-generating station, established in the

View from Cape Smokey

Cape Smokey Provincial Park

intersection with a flashing light. You can continue straight on to the Englishtown ferry at Jersey Cove or follow the Cabot Trail inland, through the communities of Tarbotvale and Tarbot. The Oregon Road leads to North River Provincial Park, where a 18-km (11.2 mi) hiking trail winds through a steep river gorge to the 32-m (104-ft) waterfalls. Various small trails lead to swimming holes and salmon fishing pools. Large rock piles along the trail are all that remain of farmers' efforts to clear this land. As the trail continues, it narrows considerably, increasing the level of difficulty. The waterfall is situated in a steep-sided canyon. To the right of the rest area, a small, arduous trail continues straight up the hill. For an even more dazzling view of the falls, follow this trail to the top of the mountain. Be careful not to lose your footing on the wet stones.

From the provincial park, the Cabot Trail skirts the North River to emerge finally at St. Anns Harbour. At the mouth of the harbour lie St. Anns Provincial Park and the Nova Scotia Gaelic College.

1970s when oil prices took a jump on world markets and governments turned to hydro as an alternative source of energy. Behind the silent mountains, eleven major dams drain an area of 216 sq km (134 sq mi), while the station produces an annual average of 318+ million kWh. In addition to providing a cheap source of power, the plant also guarantees the water flow into the Cheticamp River, a habitat for Atlantic salmon.

From Wreck Cove onwards, the Cabot Trail clings to the coast, weaving placidly through the communities of Birch Plain, French River, Breton Cove and Little River. At North Shore, Plaster Provincial Park has a hiking trail to a cobblestone beach. From here, you can see the Hertford and Ciboux islands, known locally as the Bird Islands. Farther on, at Tarbotvale, there is an

Wreck Cove General Store

Wild Things artisan's shop at Tarbotvale

COLAISDE NA GÀIDHLIG - NOVA SCOTIA GAELIC COLLEGE, ST. ANNS

The area around St. Anns Bay has long been a centre of the Gaelic language and Celtic culture in North America. Settlement in this area dates to 1820, when Reverend Norman MacLeod arrived with a small band of followers. Enroute to Ohio, they had been storm-driven to St. Anns Bay and chose to remain there. At first, the community was a flourishing centre of farming, fishing and shipbuilding. By 1851, however, two years of successive crop failure had induced the seventy-year-old pastor to seek fairer fields. Between 1851 and 1859, six ships left for Australia and New Zealand carrying over 800 people. Today, the community of St. Anns still maintains contact with its sister community in Waipu, New Zealand.

In spite of the exodus to New Zealand, enough people remained to ensure that the Gaelic language and Celtic culture endured. Cultural survival was further assured in 1938, when the Rev. A.W.R. MacKenzie established a school devoted to the cause. Set against a backdrop of lake and mountains, the Gaelic College provides a natural stage for the performers who gather here each summer for the college's six-week summer school. Thanks to the Gaelic College, successive generations of children learn the traditional arts of piping, dancing,

fiddling, drumming, celtic harp and weaving. Taught by famous artists and performers, the classes are often held outdoors for the benefit of the general public. In the early summer, KitchenFest! features local musicians, fiddlers, storytellers and dancers in venues across Cape Breton. Visitors also enjoy the Great Hall of the Clans, which explores the history of the clans and their tartans. Nearby, the college gift shop offers a large selection of handcrafts and Scottish tartans, with kilts made to fit.

ENGLISHTOWN

F rom the Gaelic College, the road continues on to rejoin the Trans-Canada Highway (route 105). The Cabot Trail ends here, just south of Baddeck. By now, however, you may find yourself caught by Cape Breton's magic. And there is still so much left to explore. To the north, fewer than 5 km (3 mi) away, lies the village of Englishtown, located off the Trans-Canada on St. Anns Harbour. Momentous events

St. Anns Look-off

the colonization rights to Acadia. Landing on Cape Breton's east coast with sixty Scottish colonists, Stewart immediately began building Fort Rosemar.

The New World proved to be unforgiving. Sir James committed a single mistake. Upon his arrival, he began to collect a full tenth of the catch from passing French fishermen, some of whom had been fishing in the area since before he was born.

occurred in this tiny corner of the world, events that influenced the course of North American history.

The history of St. Anns Bay begins with two brothers. One was saintly, the other worldly. One coveted men's souls, the other their fortunes.

The Daniel brothers came to Cape Breton from France in the 1630s. Father Antoine Daniel was a Jesuit missionary, who devoted himself to ministering to the local Mi'kmaq. St. Anthony Daniel Church, in Sydney, is named in his honour. His brother, Captain Charles Daniel, sailed the seas around Cape Breton, seizing fortune on the wing. His chance came in 1629, with the arrival of Sir James Stewart, Lord Ochiltree. Eight years earlier, the British monarch had granted Stewart's family

Unfortunately for Sir James, the fishermen complained to Captain Daniel. Swooping down on Stewart's fort, Daniel burned the buildings, carrying both loot and colonists off to St. Anns Bay. There, they were set the task of building a new fort, before being shipped back to Scotland.

Sir James Stewart's dreams of empire had lasted just three short months. Meanwhile, on the shores of St. Anns Bay,

MacAskill Museum

MacAskill Museum: exterior (above); interior (right)

humble farmer's son and the most powerful woman in the world?

MacAskill's career was cut short when, on a bet, he attempted to lift a giant anchor. As MacAskill placed the anchor back on the pier, it slipped and one of the flukes pinned him to the ground, causing internal injuries. Broken, he returned to St. Anns Bay, to the delight of the village children. For the

Antoine Daniel preached the gospel of Christ, while his brother Charles guarded the entrance to the Gulf of St. Lawrence, protecting it from British ships. Known as Port Dauphin (after the French king's eldest son), St. Anns served as France's Atlantic base until the construction of Fortress Louisbourg in 1720.

Together the Daniel brothers had done their best to safeguard the island for king and church. In the end, however, it was Sir James who can be said to have triumphed. Two centuries after his death, Stewart's dream of seeing the island peopled with Scots came true.

As we know, many of the Scots swept onto the shores of Cape Breton in the 1800s landed here, in St. Anns Bay. One of these became one of the most famous men of his time. Angus MacAskill, known as "The Cape Breton Giant," was born in 1825 in Bernera, one of the Hebrides islands off the coast of Scotland. MacAskill came to Cape Breton as a small child and grew up on his family's farm. Like many Cape Bretoners before and since, he left the island as a young man, to seek his fortune in the "Boston States." Joining Barnum's Circus, he was teamed with Tom Thumb and invited to appear before Queen Victoria. What did they talk about, the 7-foot 9-inch giant and the tiny queen; the

rest of his short life, this "gentle giant" remained in his home village. He is there still. To see his grave, walk up the hill, to the cemetery near the ferry dock. Farther on, near the Trans-Canada, a museum run by family members continues to fascinate children with MacAskill's specially made clothing and furniture.

Fairy Hole

Few people are lucky enough to have their gods walk among them. Yet Kluskap, hero of the Mi'kmaw nation, once resided in a small cave below the sacred mountain.

To reach Kluskap's Cave, take the New Campbellton Road, an unpaved road located on the hairpin turn on the eastern slope of Kellys Mountain. Follow the road to the end, a distance of 13 km (8 mi), then park on the side of the road. A small shed on your left marks the beginning of the trail, leading uphill into the woods.

The trail begins as a pleasant, undulating walk through sunlit forests. The floor is covered with moss and varieties of fern. Appropriately for a trail named Fairy Hole, several varieties of toadstools line the path. After 2.4 km (1.5 mi) of continuous walking, you will come to a brook. Turn right on the bank and follow the brook to the coast. As it approaches the beach, walking becomes more difficult. Depending on the time of year, you may find yourself criss-crossing the river, jumping from stone to stone. A series of small pools makes fine paddling for children. The trail emerges from the narrow gorge onto a small, protected beach. The Bird Islands lie straight ahead.

For the Mi'kmaq, these islands are all that remains of Kluskap's canoe. Long ago, in the act of giving birth to a prophet, Nova Scotia was both changed and consecrated. The Bras d'Or Lakes were created during Kluskap's wild pursuit of a giant beaver. To escape, the beaver burrowed under the land, creating the channels that join the lakes to the sea. The pursuit continued onto the mainland, where Kluskap dug a channel to flush out the beaver. Today, that channel is known as Minas Basin.

Fashioned by the Creator, Kluskap was invested with all the passions of humanity and like his people, he had to live with the results. He did not like to be laughed at. One day, while out fishing, Kluskap saw two maidens watching him from the shore. Leaping from the canoe, the mighty hunter broke it into two pieces. The girls' laughter rushed across the water, so enraging him that he turned the girls to stone. They endure to this day, two sentinels at the door of his cave. The broken canoe became the Bird Islands.

Kluskap's Cave is located just behind the large boulder, to your right. Even with the aid of the ropes secured into the rock, the climb is difficult. It is best to time your visit for low tide, when the rock can be skirted by wading through the water. DO NOT ENTER THE CAVE. Although the entrance is wide, the inner chambers are crumbling.

The Mi'kmaq still pay tribute to Kluskap, leaving tobacco and eels on the stone table in front of his old home. His secrets lie buried in the oral tradition, accessible only to Mi'kmaw speakers. To truly understand Kluskap is to sit at the feet of a great storyteller, over the course of many nights, listening to tales in one's own tongue. The Kluskap tales teach morality and ethics while recounting stories about mythical creatures of land and sea. When a Mi'kmaw hunter asks Kluskap for long life, he is turned into a twisted cedar tree.

Kluskap left the island long ago. After foretelling the arrival of the Europeans, he took his mother and brother into the west. It is said that any who seek him will find him, though the way is both difficult and long. He will return in the hour of his people's greatest need.

Bird Island Boat Tours

By now you will certainly have seen one of Cape Breton's most cherished symbols, the "MacPuffin." Dressed in cromack and bonnet, this saucy bird graces restaurant menus, t-shirts and motels. Boat tours to Bird Island offer the chance to see the Atlantic Puffin in its natural habitat. One operator offers tours from Englishtown; the other can be found across Seal Island Bridge, off exit 14 to Big Bras d'Or. From mid-May to mid-October, passengers board tour boats for a narrated tour of the Hertford and Ciboux Islands. The boats are approved by Canadian Coast Guard. The islands are also home to grey seals, razor-billed auks, black guillemots, kittiwakes, cormorants, gulls and bald eagles.

Bald eagles

NORTH SYDNEY AND SYDNEY MINES

Route 105 continues across Kellys Mountain, to the Seal Island Bridge. Completed in 1961, this bridge replaced the ferry service that ran between Ross Ferry and Big Harbour. From here, the Trans-Canada leads us into the heart of industrial Cape Breton, the island's most heavily populated district. Now known as the Cape Breton Regional Municipality, it incorporates the former towns of Sydney Mines, North Sydney, Sydney, Glace Bay, New Waterford, Dominion and Louisbourg.

Cape Breton historian Robert Morgan has said that

Cape Breton was initially a place to send unwanted populations. This was certainly true of the Loyalists. With the American Revolution, Britain needed a place in which to settle the thousands of people who wished to continue living under British rule. Known as the Loyalists, they gathered in the port of New York waiting to embark on a new life in British territory. Approximately 40,000 settled in Nova Scotia and New Brunswick. Under the direction of royal surveyor J.F.W. Desbarres, several hundred settled in the area around Spanish Bay, known today as Sydney Harbour. Others settled in the broad river valleys around Baddeck and Mabou.

Theirs was not the typical pioneer experience. The Loyalists came from all walks of life. Many were artisans from the bustling cities of the Thirteen Colonies. Some were free men and women of African descent, who had served as soldiers and laundresses behind British lines. Others were slaves, brought to Nova Scotia by their owners.

Many of the Loyalists who came to Nova Scotia were skilled professionals, having left promising careers in the

Kellys Mountain

Big Bras d'Or

army, the law and in medicine. Determined to recreate their former life of ease, they brought along their servants, furnishings and capital. From the Nova Scotia government they demanded, and received, extra supplies, a regiment for their protection and a voice in their government.

From stately homes on quiet tree-lined streets, the Loyalists prepared to resume their professions. In North Sydney, sea captains and merchant princes channelled foodstuffs and other agricultural products to the fishermen of Newfoundland. During the age of sail, the harbour was filled with vessels of all sizes. Gradually these were replaced by steamships. By 1878, a regular ferry service was established between North Sydney and Newfoundland. North Sydney's role as a communications centre was further consolidated when Western Union set up an office here. It was from North Sydney, in 1909, that the world first learned of Admiral Peary's arrival at the North Pole. Later, during World War Two, the area once again played a crucial role in world events as convoys assembled in its harbour, in preparation for the crossing to England. For many local people, the most tragic event of the war occurred on October 14,

1942, when the Newfoundland passenger ferry SS *Caribou* was torpedoed by a German U-boat, with great loss of life.

Today North Sydney remains the home of the Newfoundland ferry service. Two vessels offers year-round service, but check ahead if the weather is bad. In addition to exploring the fine beaches and seaside parks, visitors enjoy the facilities at the Northern Yacht Club and the eighteen-hole Seaview Golf and Country Club. The area also offers more pastoral pleasures. Each year, in August, farmers exhibit their livestock and vegetables at the Cape Breton County Farmers' Exhibition. In the pie and flower competitions, local women still vie for the blue ribbon.

From North Sydney it's a short distance north along the harbour to Sydney Mines. Here on the northwestern edge of the Sydney coal field, residents have traditionally earned their living from mining. One of the town's most interesting features is the Old Sydney Mines Post Office. Built in 1904 and renovated in 1989, this heritage property is a fine example of the gothic architecture so popular during the industrial age.

HISTORIC SYDNEY LANDMARKS

From Sydney Mines, take exit 20 to route 125. This will lead you to downtown Sydney. Founded by Loyalists in 1785, the city was named in honour of Lord Sydney, Secretary of State for the Colonies. As British patriots in an age of revolution, the town's American-born founders named the principal streets after the British Royal family — George Street, Charlotte Street and Prince Street.

Cossit House

In the late eighteenth century, Sydney was a garrison town. To protect the harbour, regiments were stationed in Barrack Park in the north end of the city, known today as Victoria Park. Sydney's north end also contains a number of buildings constructed during the early Loyalist period. The city's oldest building is Cossit House, built in 1787 by Cape Breton's first Protestant minister, the Reverend Ranna Cossit. He and his wife, the former Thankful Brooks, left New Hampshire with their family of seven children. Six more children were born in Sydney, the whole family growing up in this small, one-and-a-half story building, with its gabled roof. We may wonder at the riotous family life that must have gone inside. Yet this was normal for the period, when children slept in the attic — several to a bed — and were encouraged to spend much of their time outdoors.

Today, Cossit House is the property of the Nova Scotia Museum and is operated by the Old Sydney Society. It has been restored, as closely as possible, to its original state. The period furnishing is based on an inventory of Ranna Cossit's estate, completed at the time of his death in 1815.

For the Reverend Cossit, it was a short walk from his house to St. George's Anglican Church. Erected in 1785 by engineers from the 33rd Regiment, this church was built with stone salvaged from the Fortress of Louisbourg. As both garrison chapel and parish church, St. George's was the gathering

St. Patrick's Church

Jost House

place for the cream of Loyalist society. Lord Nelson, victor of the Battle of Trafalgar, attended services here in 1805. Noting the absence of a bishop's chair, he presented the church with a Chippendale chair from the wardroom of his ship. Today, in Portsmouth, England, the matching chairs can still be seen on Nelson's ship, HMS *Victory*.

The town's Roman Catholics worshipped in St. Patrick's Church, now a museum located on the Esplanade. Built in 1828, to replace an earlier church destroyed by fire, it is the oldest-standing Catholic church in Cape Breton. At one point during its history, it served as the parish church for the newly arrived Lebanese immigrants. Throughout the 1950s, it belonged to the Ancient Order of Hibernians, until its purchase by the Old Sydney Society. The museum is one of the six buildings featured in the society's guided walking tours of the city.

One of the most popular houses on this tour is Jost House, located on 54 Charlotte Street. The house is furnished to represent several different periods in the history of Sydney. The basement, complete with cooking hearth and bake-oven, dates to the late eighteenth century, when the building was the property of merchant and shipowner Samuel Sparrow. The furnishings on the ground floor were in vogue during the lifetime of Thomas Jost, a Halifax merchant who purchased the property in 1836. Upstairs, an apothecary dates to the early twentieth century. A marine room explores the role that the sea and ships played throughout the city's history.

Other houses, not open to the public, provide interesting stops on the tour of Sydney's old north end. No. 3 Charlotte Street, built in 1897, was the home of songstress Rita MacNeil. No. 12 Charlotte Street (1897) was the original site of the Jubilee Methodist Church, while No. 25 (1831) housed the courthouse and jail. No. 90 Charlotte Street (1790) was the residence of Governor Nicholas Nepean. The story is told of a "fairy child" who once appeared to play with the children of the house, then vanished down the stairwell.

To learn more about the history of old Sydney, visit the Sydney Museum, located at 173 Charlotte Street. Formerly the museum was located at 225 George Street, at the building known as the Lyceum. It was constructed as an opera house, in 1904. (The Von Trapp Family, of "The Sound of Music" fame, once appeared here.) After extensive renovations in the 1950s, the building served as a junior college of St. Francis Xavier University. Today, it is still used by Sydney's artistic and theatrical communities.

The Evolution of a City

Sydney's waterfront has changed much since the early days. As the capital of Cape Breton Colony from 1785 until 1820, Sydney was a sleepy little government town. At the end of this period, however, a series of shocks changed the city forever. At the request of authorities in Halifax, Cape Breton was annexed to Nova Scotia, losing much of its political power in the process. Meanwhile, Scottish immigration was in full swing bringing a flood of Gaelic to the area.

Another major influence on the city was the development of coal mines and steel production by industrialists from the United States and Britain. This new elite helped found the Royal Cape Breton Yacht Club. The club received its charter from King Edward VII in person. Moored offshore while on a tour of Canada, the king could not visit any but a royal yacht club. To solve the problem, he simply created one. Today, the Royal Cape Breton is one of two yacht clubs in Sydney. The Dobson Yacht Club is located across the harbour, in Westmount. Reflecting today's more democratic climate, both clubs now serve the general Cape Breton community and are open to visitors.

While the company bosses were wined and dined in

their clubs and hotels, a very different kind of society was emerging elsewhere in Sydney. As immigrants poured in to work the mines and the mills, a new city began to envelop the original core in the north end. Ukrainians, Italians, Poles, African-Americans, Lebanese and Jews arrived, bringing with them new values and new lifestyles. Suddenly, the small patrician loyalist town was transformed into a large, multi-ethnic, multilingual community, with everyone bound together by a single commodity: steel. Sydney became known as the "steel city," with many of its people settled in company homes in Whitney Pier.

Each group retained elements of its cooking, language, music and faith. There are currently eight churches in the small community of Whitney Pier. Of these, the Holy Ghost Ukrainian Church is the only one of its kind east of Montreal while St. Philip's is Canada's only African Orthodox Church. St. Mary's Church serves the large Polish community, while St. Nicholas' parish ministers to those of Italian descent. To learn more about the community's cultural history, visit the Whitney Pier Historical Society Museum on 88 Mount Pleasant Street. Housed in a former synagogue, the museum is open from late May to October.

Sydney is a favoured port of call for many of the world's largest cruise lines, and so visitor facilities have been built on the government wharf to accommodate the many thousands of cruise ship passengers, as well as other tourists, who visit each year. Built to provide information and enjoyment to everyone who visits, the dock features an extensive information centre and interpretive exhibit, craft market, craft workshop and retail shops, food and beverage service and, of course, a Cape Breton music venue. For all those who can't quite leave it all behind, there's a free internet cafe. The adjacent waterfront boardwalk is a fine place for a stroll.

At Cape Breton University, located on the Sydney-Glace Bay highway, the Beaton Institute also contains a wealth of information on Cape Breton history in the form of books, paintings, manuscripts, microfiche, audio and video tapes and maps. The collection of approximately 50,000 photographs contains many interesting images of the island's early industrial period. All those interested in researching their roots should explore the institute's extensive genealogical archives.

During the industrial age, the multicultural blend helped produce a Cape Breton culture. A hard life in the mines and mills has given the residents an ironic, quirky sense of humour. Action Week, celebrated in the first week of August, is a time for area residents to come together and celebrate this common heritage. Past events have included farmers markets, pancake breakfasts, buskers festivals, craft festivals and harbour cruises.

Blast Furnace, Sydney

LOUISBOURG

F rom Sydney's route 125, take exit 8 onto route 22,
for the thirty-minute drive to the modern town
of Louisbourg. The eighteenth-century fortress of
Louisbourg lies just beyond, at the end of the main street.
On a summer's day, with the sun glinting off the fortress
stones, it's easy to appreciate the French choice of this fine
harbour. But on a cold, foggy day, it's hard to imagine what
could have brought them to this place. The land is so rocky
and boggy that even a turnip is hard pressed to survive.
Were they fools or dreamers, the people who first settled
here? The answer is neither. The French were entrepre-

neurs. Located close to the fishing grounds, Louisbourg was
as fine a place as any to make a fortune.

A visit to the Fortress of Louisbourg begins at the visitor reception centre. Take along a thick sweater and warm
shoes. The weather may suddenly turn chill, with fog banks
sweeping in off the ocean. In fog, remember to switch off
your headlights before leaving the car. Park wardens regularly rescue motorists stranded by a dead battery.

At the visitors reception centre, taking some time to view
the exhibits and slide show will enhance the experience.
The cost of admission covers the bus ride to the fortress,

King's Bastion at sunrise

Cannons behind the forge

An officer at Louisbourg

entrance to the animated buildings and guided walking tours. Tickets purchased two hours before closing are valid for the next day. Family passes are also available. Full services are available from July through early September, with reduced services in the months of May to June, and September to October. Guided, outside walking tours are also available in winter, with prior arrangement.

From the visitors reception centre, it is a short bus ride into the eighteenth century. Visitors are deposited at the home of Jeanne Galbarette and her husband, Georges Desroches. In a sense, the pair were typical of the people who settled Louisbourg: hardy fishing folk, lucky enough to own a fine, cobbled stretch of beach, suitable for drying the fish. Here, Jeanne Galbarette served ragoût and spruce beer to the Basque fishermen who worked for them, while her husband, Georges, busied himself with their shipbuilding business. Theirs was a hard life, typical of the fishing proprietors who lined the harbour. In another way, however, Jeanne and Georges were not typical at all. At the time of their marriage she was sixty-nine and he was twenty-eight. Both were possessed of an uncommon courage. Together, this pair braved war and occupation, choosing to stay on their property even after the fortress had fallen to the English.

The atmosphere of war is evident as soon as you enter the fortress. The year is 1744, the summer before the first attack by New England and British forces. With war in the air and the town full of spies, the soldiers are understandably jumpy. Up on the hill, in the citadel, Governor Duquesnel commands a force of over 600 recruits and their officers, few of whom have had combat experience. Already, just twenty years after their construction, the mighty walls are crumbling, victims of the fog and salt spray. Unwilling to put the walls to the test of British cannon, engineers are counting on the strength of their seaward defenses. Just offshore the guns of the island battery are trained on the entrance to the harbour. At the harbour's far end, the tiny, exquisite fortress known as the Royal Battery stands ready to meet a full frontal attack. It's an attack that has never come. In 1745, New England soldiers emerged from the hills just behind the Royal Battery, approaching from its most vulnerable side. They took it without firing a single shot. From there, they trained their guns on the long curtain wall, jarring it with each blow. Although the soldiers inside fought bravely, it was a battle they could not hope to win.

Louisbourg fell, rose again, and fell once more. After the second siege, the British took no chances: in 1760, the fortress walls were blown up and the stones carted away. Louisbourg seemed doomed to lie forever under piles of rubble and meadow grass. Yet two hundred years later, it became the focus of a vast, reconstruction project undertaken by the Canadian government. Today, visitors can once again gaze on its walls and join in the town life. One of the best times to visit is in late August when the fortress celebrates the feast

Engineer's Garden

Louis IX of France. Garden parties feature ladies in delicate silk dresses, eating dainties shipped in from France. Fortress children run through the streets, chasing hoops and dancing to the tune of the hurdy-gurdy. In the chapel, a Te Deum provides a more solemn note, raising thanks to God for the fishery and praying for the safety of men at sea. Best of all are the fireworks, when the long curtain wall is covered in a shower of brilliant sparks. Afterward, with the flames of the giant bonfire licking the sky, fortress musicians sing old French songs, responding again and again to the calls for "*Alouette*," or "*Au claire de la lune.*"

As you proceed toward the modern town of Louisbourg, tracing your steps forward in time, linger for a moment at the end of the nineteenth century. (At this time, the town was known by its English spelling, "Louisburg.") During Cape Breton's coal boom, Louisbourg's ice-free harbour served as the central point for all the coal shipped from the island. Under the direction of industrialist H. M. Whitney, the Sydney and Louisburg Railway was built to link all the collieries to Louisbourg. Construction of the line was completed in 1895.

As one of the most modern railways in Canada, the S & L was built at a time when people's faith in the benefits of progress and technology was undimmed. The Louisbourg economy was booming, yet residents still enjoyed all the amenities of life in a small town. Passengers on the S & L regularly took the train into the country for picnics. Engineers kept a close watch out for hunters and blueberry pickers, hitching a ride home at the end of the day.

During the two world wars, Louisbourg was an important convoy point for fleets preparing to cross the Atlantic. Afterwards, as the airplane and automobile gained ascendency, Louisbourg's role as a port diminished somewhat. With oil proving a more efficient and cheaper fuel, coal was no longer king. By the 1960s, the S & L was an anachronism. The station is now a museum containing two furnished coach cars, a caboose, an oil car and a freight car, as well as several small, gas-powered and manual repair crew vehicles. Inside, visitors can tour the stationmaster's office and living quarters.

Today, Louisbourg's people seek other ways to make a living. Fishing boats still leave for the grounds each morning, harvesting snow crab and lobster. Increasingly, however, townspeople are exploring new roles, in the fields of culture, tourism and the performing arts. The Louisbourg Playhouse was originally constructed as part of the set for the Disney movie, *Squanto: A Warrior's Tale*, made in Louisbourg in 1993. Now located on Aberdeen Street, the playhouse is a showcase for local talent. In August, the crab festival is another excellent place to see the newest talents while enjoying a traditional community dinner of snow crab, potato salad and coleslaw. The event takes place at various venues in Louisbourg. Complete with boat launch and floating dock, this is one of the most exciting places to be in a Cape Breton summer.

Miners' Museum, Glace Bay

From Louisbourg, visitors can return to Sydney, or take the scenic Marconi Trail (route 255) to Glace Bay. Driving time is approximately one hour, proceeding along the shore through the village of Main-à-Dieu. Stand anywhere on the coast, look out to sea, and you are in a direct line to France. It is here, near Baleine, that we find the tiny promontory of land known as "Cape Breton," from which the island takes its name. Located on the same latitude as the French cities of Rochefort and La Rochelle, this cape was a natural landfall for Breton fishermen.

Winding along the coast towards Glace Bay, the Marconi Trail passes through the village of Port Morien, the site of Cape Breton's first coal mine. Port Morien is located on the vast Sydney

House in the Miners' Village, part of the Miners' Museum

coalfield, which extends almost as far as Newfoundland. The coal seams, some over 4 m (13 ft) thick, were created by geological activity that began over 300 million years ago as peat deposits were buried under layers of sediment. These seams were discovered by the French in 1720. Suffering intensely from the cold, the French in Louisbourg were overjoyed to find such an efficient source of fuel. Gradually, their draughty fireplaces were replaced with snug, glowing stoves.

In modern Port Morien, a cairn marks the location of this early mine. Later, after the British conquest of

Louisbourg in 1745, British troops also mined the exposed seams. Upon assuming control in Cape Breton, the British let the seams go unexploited. Afraid that island mines would compete with the home industry for coal markets, the British government closed the island to settlement. Ironically, it was the entanglements of the Royal Family that finally permitted the extraction of Cape Breton's coal.

George III had granted the Nova Scotia mines to his son, the Duke of York. Deep in debt to his jeweller, the duke leased the mines to the General Mining Association of Britain. Later,

the Reciprocity Treaty with the United States and the demand created by the Civil War drew the attention of American industrialists to the tiny, coal-rich island. In 1897, the American entrepreneur H.M. Whitney created the Dominion

A tour at the Miners' Museum

Entrance to French Mine, Morien

Savoy Theatre

hardhats, and with a retired coalminer as guide, visitors descend for a twenty-minute trip into the Ocean Deeps Colliery, a "room and pillar" mine of the type used in the early 1930s. To highlight the contrasts between modern and historic mining, an interactive exhibit offers a simulated trip into the Phalen Colliery. Sitting in a man rake, visitors are 'transported' underground with the use of modern technology.

Another attraction is the Miners' Museum Little Theatre where the Men of the Deeps give regular musical performances throughout the summer. Coalminers all, these choral singers have performed throughout Canada, the United States and in Japan. Some of their most memorable performances have been with Rita MacNeil, in their rendition of her song, "Working Man."

Outside, take a stroll through the Miners' Village, which consists of a reconstructed miner's house, a company store and a restaurant. As if in compensation for the hardships suffered underground, the miners and their families developed a rich community life. Glace Bay sports teams became famous throughout Canada. Today, the Glace Bay Heritage Museum, located on McKeen Street, commemorates the unique role that sports played in the town's development.

Music and theatre also lightened the lives of the people. The Donkin Citizens Brass Band has performed continuously since 1919, winning many awards. Glace Bay's Savoy Theatre, built in 1927, was respectively a music hall, vaudeville theatre and silent movie theatre. Today, the Savoy continues to offer live stage performances. Rita MacNeil, the Rankin Family, the Barra MacNeils, Natalie MacMaster, Winnie Chafe and the Men of the Deeps have all performed there.

Coal Company, gathering the ownership of numerous small, private mines into his hands.

The impact this company had on the life of Cape Bretoners is immeasurable. Until then, many of the new immigrants were farmers, trying to wrest a living from the rocky soil and short growing season. Now, from all over the island, young men and women from these farms were drawn to the mining towns. Though the work was hard, the pay was regular.

The towns also drew young Irish labourers from the Newfoundland fishery. Since the seventeenth century, thousands of young men and women had set out from the Irish port of Waterford, bound for St. John's. Eventually they formed a large Irish-Catholic community in that city. Later, they headed for Cape Breton's mining towns. One of these was named New Waterford, in honour of the Irish city. Glace Bay was named for the fields of drift ice that clog its harbour each spring. (*Glace* is French for ice.)

Other new towns, including Donkin, Reserve Mines, Gardiner Mines and Dominion, also sprang up on the face of the coal field. During World War One, over 12,000 miners produced one-third of the nation's coal, with twelve collieries located in the town of Glace Bay alone. Today miners and their families grieve over the closure of the mines.

In Glace Bay, at Quarry Point, the Miners' Museum traces the development of the mining industry in Cape Breton, from its beginnings to the present day. Donning

BEN EOIN AND BIG POND

From Sydney, take exit 6 to route 4, enroute to St. Peters. First built in 1788, this is one of the oldest highways in Nova Scotia. Its purpose was to move troops between the Loyalist settlements of Sydney and St. Peters.

From Sydney, there is still a continual movement along this road. On the East Bay side of the Bras d'Or Lakes, Ben Eoin is another of Cape Breton's most popular beaches and resorts. Residents drive out to camp, swim or watch the eagles that nest in the area.

Customers at Rita's Tea Room

Down the road, the Big Pond Summer Festival draws large crowds. In addition to musical entertainment, the festival offers such traditional activities as strawberry festivals and the blessing of the fleet. Tarabish players from around the island eagerly look forward to the annual tournament. A form of bridge, tarabish is widely known as a Cape Breton game. It is, however, based on a card game first brought to the island by Lebanese peddlers. Setting out from Sydney, these young men stayed in Scottish homes along their routes. Throughout the summer nights, they taught their hosts this card game, and learned some Gaelic in return. Today, in Sydney, affluent Lebanese businessmen still remember those days on the road.

Situated on the Bras d'Or Lakes, Big Pond is a major breeding area for bald eagles. Populations are so healthy that Cape Breton recently responded to an appeal by American biologists to resettle young eaglets in Western Massachusetts.

Big Pond is also the childhood home of international singing artist Rita MacNeil. Rita's Tea Room was originally a one-room schoolhouse, built in 1938. Although she did not attend this school, Rita purchased the property in 1982, as a place to relax between tours. Each time she returned to the stage, Rita repeated the old Cape Breton refrain, "If you're ever in Cape Breton, drop by for a cup of tea." The tea room closed in 2019. Her fans — thousands of them — took her at her word. To meet the demand, Rita converted her home into a tea room, offering home-baked goods and her own special blend of tea. The tea room also has an interesting exhibit of Rita's life and career, while the gift shop sells customized souvenirs, clothing, Cape Breton music and Rita's own signature china. Now an important addition to the area's economy, the tea room welcomes 35,000 visitors annually. Before her death in 2013, the star herself used to drop in from time to time to chat with customers. The tea room is open from late May to the end of the Celtic Colours Festival in October, seven days a week, 9 am to 7 pm.

St. Peters, Dundee Resort Golf Course and Isle Madame

St. Peters Canal

From Rita's Tea Room, continue along route 4, through the Mi'kmaw community of Chapel Island. Known in Mi'kmaw as Potlotek or "Place of Light," this is the spiritual centre of the Mi'kmaw nation. According to the Mi'kmaw oral tradition, the island was initially an ancient burial ground. Later, Father Maillard, a French priest, established a Roman Catholic mission on the island. To this day, the Mi'kmaw nation still gathers at Chapel Island every July 26 to celebrate the feast day of St. Anne, their patron saint. The stone that bears St. Anne's statue is said to be Father Maillard's altar.

From Chapel Island, the road continues on to St. Peters, known as the "gateway to the Bras d'Or Lakes." The narrow isthmus that separates the Bras d'Or Lakes from the Atlantic Ocean was a traditional portage route for the local Mi'kmaq. In the French period, Mi'kmaw hunters would bring their canoes, loaded with furs, to the harbour, where traders waited. The famous French trader Nicholas Denys established a trading, fishing and lumbering station here in

Inside the Denys Museum

For both French and Mi'kmaq, the fall of Louisbourg in 1758 signalled the end of a way of life. In the aftermath of war, all of the Mi'kmaw energies were focussed on survival, while the majority of the French and Acadian residents were deported. In the 1780s, the village of St. Peters was settled by Loyalists. Like their French predecessors, they concentrated on farming and fishing. With the advent of the industrial age, however, St. Peters resumed its historic role as the gateway to the Bras d'Or Lakes. This time the commodity was coal, not furs. In 1854, a canal was constructed to allow for the transportation of coal from the lakes to the mainland.

the mid-seventeenth century. Known as Fort Saint Pierre, after his patron saint, the fort was the early capital of Denys' fief, which stretched from Canso to Gaspé. It was in this fort, in 1655, that Nicholas Denys' son Richard was born.

After Fort St. Pierre burned to the ground in the winter of 1668–69, Denys and his family moved to Nepisiguit (now Bathurst, New Brunswick). There, he settled down to write his memoirs, which were published in France in 1672. Entitled *The Description and Natural History of the Coasts of North America (Acadia)*, the book provides a detailed description of Cape Breton and its people. Both father and son maintained cordial relations with the Mi'kmaq. Nicholas was affectionately known as "big beard," while his son Richard married into the Mi'kmaw nation. He and his wife, Anne Patarabego, had two children, however Richard died when the children were still quite young. Their fate remains unknown.

After the departure of Nicholas and Richard Denys, the Cape Breton Mi'kmaq continued to welcome the occasional fisherman and fur trader. Official French settlement was not resumed until 1713, with the establishment of Louisbourg. Now known as Port Toulouse, St. Peters was an important meeting place for the French and Mi'kmaq. Each summer, the French honoured their Mi'kmaw allies with medals, guns and ammunition. The area became the political centre of the Mi'kmaw nation in 1749 when Grand Chief Tomah Denys moved to Chapel Island from the mainland.

Although St. Peters never became a major transportation centre, the double-gate tidal lock canal continues to provide access to the Bras d'Or Lakes. Deep, clean and fog-free, this vast inland sea is the perfect venue for sailing and boating. Measuring 91.44 m x 14.45 m (300 ft x 47.4 ft), the canal can accommodate vessels with a 4.88 m (16 ft) draught. (Twelve-hour advance notice is required for passage between the months of October and May.)

Now a heritage canal, the site offers outdoor exhibits in French, English and Mi'kmaw. On the ocean end of the canal, Battery Provincial Park is a picnic and camping area, with views of the ocean. Nearby, the Nicholas Denys Museum occupies the site of the seventeenth-century fort. Through interpretative exhibits, photographs and historical artifacts, the museum explores the entire history of the community, from Denys' time through the nineteenth century.

Along the main street of St. Peters, summer visitors can explore the childhood home of marine photographer Wallace MacAskill, whose hand-tinted prints are exhibited in the museum. MacIssac Kiltmakers, also on the main street, specializes in handmade highland outfits for men and women, and dancers' outfits.

In addition to restaurants and accommodations, St. Peters also offers banking facilities, an RCMP detachment,

a liquor store and a marina. Those who plan on spending some time in the village should tune in to the local cable TV channel, where programs produced by local students offer a piquant window on community life.

From St. Peters, provincial route 104 proceeds directly to the Canso Causeway, with driving time approximately one hour. There are, however, two alternate routes. In St. Peters, a right turn on Pepperell Street passes through the communities of Sampsonville, French Cove and St. George's Channel, to Dundee. Situated high over the beautiful West Bay, the Dundee Resort Golf Course ranks as the second-highest slope in the province. Electric golf carts are available.

The other alternate route is to proceed to the Acadian communities on Isle Madame, along the Fleur-de-Lis Trail. From route 104, take the exit to Louisdale, then cross the Lennox Passage Bridge to Isle Madame. Named for one of the ladies of the French royal family, Isle Madame was an important fishing outport in the first half of the eighteenth century. From here, numerous fishing stations supplied cod to the Fortress of Louisbourg, for transshipment to the Caribbean.

The road from Louisdale winds through several large, Acadian communities, including West Arichat, Arichat, Petit-de-Grat, Little Anse and D'Escousse. Driving time is less than an hour. Arichat is the shiretown of Richmond County and the original home of St. Francis Xavier University, founded here in 1853. Two years later, the

Marache Point lighthouse

the rugged shore and over headlands is truly enjoyable. It's easy to imagine a time when pioneer families struggled to survive here, and shipwrecks offshore were not uncommon. Pilot and minke whales are often sighted, as well as the occasional porpoise. The entire trail is approximately 16 km (10 mi) return, but hikers can turn back at any time.

To get to the trailhead (and picnic area) at Boudreauville, drive through the village of Petit-de-Grat, but instead of crossing the bridge, keep straight to Boudreauville. When you reach the gravel road, follow it to the parking area.

university was moved to Antigonish, on the mainland.

Arichat was first settled by Acadians in the early eighteenth century. Although the Acadians were deported after the fall of Louisbourg in 1758, they were permitted to return in 1763, largely due to the petitions of the Jersey fishing merchants. During the time the Acadians fished for the Jersey merchants, all business was done on credit, leaving the people deep in debt. In the end, however, the Acadians freed themselves from this economic bondage and established their own cooperatives.

Located on the lower road off route 206, LeNoir Forge recalls a time when communities such as Arichat, isolated for much of the year, relied on small, independent artisans to provide goods and services. In addition to making nails, wagon wheels, horseshoes and other homely objects, the blacksmith also spent much of his time mending broken items.

The oldest settlement on Isle Madame, Petit-de-Grat was an important shipbuilding centre, with architecture reflecting its seafaring past.

There is excellent hiking along the coast of Isle Madame, and the Cape Auget Ecotrail is the perfect opportunity. While the trail is no longer groomed, this hike along

From Petit-de-Grat, drive back towards Arichat, turning on to route 320 to D'Escousse. From D'Escousse, continue along the loop, back to Louisdale. From here, the highway leads directly to Port Hawkesbury, once known as Ship Harbour. Farther along the highway, the Port Hastings Historical Museum and Archives explores the area's seafaring past, as well as the construction of the Canso Causeway.

Beyond lies the causeway and the world.

D'Escousse Harbourfest

INDEX